14

CONTEMPORARY THEOLOGY

A reading guide

by

URBAN J. STEINER, O.S.B.

THE LITURGICAL PRESS
Collegeville, Minnesota

ii

TABLE OF CONTENTS

INTRODUCTION

Year after year the annual summary of book publication reveals that religion and theology are among the most productive subject fields. The Second Vatican Council with its liturgical, ecumenical, and pastoral concern has done much to add to the surge of theological publication, so that in 1964 there were no less than 1,830* new books published in this country alone.

Hence the lament of priests, students of theology and other people interested in theology — that there are so many books published that one does not know what to begin to read — is certainly understandable if not entirely justified. Ordinarily the priest is a busy person. The demands on his time are such that the pursuit of an academic discipline comes to be almost a luxury. Yet who will deny the absolute necessity for anyone thus engaged in the service of others to read if he is going to be an effective minister of the sacramental and spoken Word. If there is little enough time available for the reading of theology itself, where will one ever find the time to read the many book reviews and other media which might organize or direct ones efforts? Haphazard reading inevitably results in an unbalanced intellectual diet, or worse, in a loss of valuable time.

To avert such contingencies there have appeared in recent years theological reading guides for ministers of some denominations. For Protestant ministers in general, the faculty of Union Theological Seminary (New York) published *A Basic Bibliography for Ministers,* and revised their work in a second edition, published in 1960. The *Andover-Newton Quarterly* devoted the September, 1963, issue to a bibliography for ministers. A similar work, entitled *A Bibliography for Pastors and Theological Students,* had been published in 1957 by Southwestern Baptist Theological Seminary. To date, no comparable work has been published for the interests of Catholic priests and students of Catholic theology. From time to time bibliographies of theology are published, but these are often found among lists of other subjects, or scattered throughout various journals and periodicals. Because they have not been compiled specifically for priests and students of theology, these lists are more often than not broadly classified under "religion" and thus have been very uneven in their contents.

Having long felt the need for such a work, I have set out to provide an annotated list of current books on theology which would be of interest to students. The annotations are largely descriptive, but frequently there is also some evaluation. Basically, the scope of this list is the core of the traditional seminary curriculum, sometimes referred to as the major disciplines: sacred scripture, dogma, church history, moral and canon law. Moreover, there have emerged in recent years certain relatively new disciplines, such as psychology and sociology, which although not yet a formal part of the seminary curriculum certainly must be considered in the training of priests as well as in the ministry of experienced pastors. With this in mind, we have devoted special chapters to selections in the fields of pastoral counseling and sociology. In the spirit of the

---

*Cf. table: "American Book Trade Output — 1964," *PUBLISHERS' WEEKLY,* January 18, 1965, p. 56.

Second Vatican Council we have attempted to give a new prominence to the fields of liturgy, as well as ecumenism and pastoral theology. It is our hope that the table of contents, the general arrangement of the work with its cross references, and the annotations will serve as a reading guide, a buying guide, and to some extent as a reference guide.

While I have not limited myself to any chronological period, the books selected are usually recent publications. Originally this guide was intended to be a list of only those books which were currently in print. But owing to the uncertainty of determining precisely when a book is out of print or when it is again reprinted, such an approach would at best be only an approximation. The greater majority of the selections are listed in *Books in Print,* for 1964. Those not found listed in this source are clearly indicated by the asterisk (*) preceding the entry. While they may no longer be available from the publisher, they could possibly be obtained from bookshops or book dealers. It has been my aim to select only the most useful books under each particular subject. Multi-volume reference sets, as well as whole monographic series, have for the most part been excluded. Books in foreign languages which have not been translated into English and highly technical studies directed to specialists have also been excluded.

Bibliographical information, including the name of the author, the title, the publisher, date of publication, pagination, and price, is regularly supplied in order to enable the user of this list to identify a particular book in making purchase or loan. Titles available in paperback editions are clearly indicated. Prices are given in order to provide some general indication of cost. For foreign publications, an approximation is made on the basis of the current rate of exchange. Users of this work will of course be aware that all publishers' prices are subject to change without notice.

It would be impossible to name all those to whom I am indebted for help in finally realizing the publication of this work. Besides the theology faculty of St. John's, to whom the work is dedicated, Rev. Aquinas Sipe, O.S.B., is to be singled out for his organization of the chapter on pastoral care and counseling. I also want to express my gratitude to Professor Robert Beech, the librarian of Union Theological Seminary in New York, and to Miss Ruth Eisenhart, the head cataloger at that institution. It was the encouragement I received while studying under their direction that urged me to develop this compilation. Finally, I want to thank my confreres and colleagues, Rev. Oliver Kapsner, O.S.B. and Rev. Benjamin Stein, O.S.B. for their inspiration and for their patience with me during the months that I labored to bring my work to completion.

15 April, 1965

URBAN J. STEINER, O.S.B.
Reference Librarian
St. John's University

CONTEMPORARY
THEOLOGY

I

SACRED SCRIPTURE

A. WHOLE BIBLE
1. English Versions

THE COMPLETE BIBLE: An American Translation. Rev. ed. Chicago: University of Chicago Press, 1939. Pp. 246. $6.75.

This is the end result of many years of scholarship. The OT was translated from the original texts, the NT from the Greek of Wescott-Hort. An excellent, readable English translation.

THE HOLY BIBLE: Confraternity of Christian Doctrine. Patterson, N.J.: St. Anthony Guild Press. In progress. Vol. I: Genesis to Ruth, 1953, $3.00. Vol. III: Job to Sirach, 1955, $5.00. Vol. IV: Isaia to Malachia, 1961, $7.00.

This is an authorized translation of the OT and NT sponsored by the Episcopal Committee of the Confraternity of Christian Doctrine and prepared by the members of the Catholic Biblical Association of America. The translations are done from original texts with the use of ancient versions. The OT will be complete with the publication of Vol. II. The NT is still in preparation.

THE HOLY BIBLE: Revised Standard Version. New York: Nelson, 1953. Pp. 997+293. $6.00.

This revision has attempted to preserve all that is best English translations as they have been used through the years. It was intended for public reading, "to put the message of the Bible in simple, enduring words...."

2. Dictionaries, Concordances, Atlases

*ALLMEN, JEAN JACQUES VON. *Companion to the Bible.* New York: Oxford University Press, 1958. Pp. 479. $6.00.

Used extensively by Catholics although it was done entirely by Protestant scholars. It is a dictionary of major theological terms and ideas found in the Bible. Although directed primarily to students, it has been found to be of great benefit to the clergy in the preparation of scripturally oriented sermons.

BALY, DENIS. *Geographical Companion to the Bible.* New York: McGraw-Hill, 1963. Pp. 196. $5.95.

Most atlases in recent years have been concerned with archeology rather than geography. Here a professional geographer points out geographical factors that helped determine the ways of life, the main trade routes, and the natural battlefields in the various periods of biblical history.

CROSS, F.L., ed. *The Oxford dictionary of the Christian church.* New York: Oxford University Press, 1957. Pp. 1,492. $20.00.

A one-volume reference work for professional clergymen and educated laymen. It contains 6,000 cross-referenced articles and 4,600 biographies, and it is historical and documentary rather than sectarian.

CRUDEN, ALEXANDER. *Cruden's concordance to the Old and New Testaments.* Westwood, N.J.: Revell, 1960. Pp. 719. $5.95. Popular ed. $1.95.

A complete, unabridged edition published more than 200 years ago. A monumental work, but its three-column arrangement on each page and its fine print are not inviting.

DAVIS, JOHN D. and GEHMAN, HENRY S., edd. *The Westminster dictionary of the Bible.* 5th ed. Philadelphia: Westminster Press, 1944. Pp. 658. $6.00.

Conservative due to its age, yet accurate. The identification of place names should be checked against more recent atlases.

ELLISON, JOHN W. *Nelson's complete concordance of the Revised Standard Version of the Bible.* New York: Nelson, 1957. Pp. 2,157. $15.00.

A concordance to accommodate the wide-spread use of the R.S.V. The use of an electronic computer facilitated its compilation, but also imposed a certain limitation: while exhaustive, it is not analytical.

ENCYCLOPEDIC DICTIONARY OF THE BIBLE. A translation and adaptation of A. van den Born's Bijbels Woordenboek. 2d ed. revised, 1954-57 by Louis F. Hartman. New York: McGraw-Hill, 1963. 2,634 columns. $27.50.

Articles range in length from seven pages to a short paragraph. Authoritative and up-to-date. Perhaps the best work of its kind available in English.

GROLLENBERG, L. H. *Atlas of the Bible.* Translated and edited by J. M. H. Reid and H. H. Rowley. New York: Nelson, 1956. Pp. 165. $15.00.

Besides the maps and indexes which one usually expects to find in an atlas, this work contains more than 400 photographs which help to illustrate landscape, customs, architecture and archeology. Also valuable is the 60,000 word essay on Bible history which incorporates the latest findings of archeology. The space devoted to the NT is somewhat brief. Although the Atlas was meant to be used with the R.S.V., cross references will also make it possible to refer to it from the Douay or Knox versions. However, to refer from the Atlas back to either of these last named versions, will create some difficulty.

HASTINGS, JAMES. *Dictionary of the Bible.* Revised and edited by F. C. Grant and H. H. Rowley. New York: Scribners, 1963. Pp. 1,059. $15.00.

This revision of the classic Hastings one-volume dictionary ensures that its information is accurate and in line with present-day knowledge. It contains good maps and diagrams.

KRAELING, EMIL G. H. *Rand McNally Bible atlas.* Chicago: Rand McNally, 1956. Pp. 487. $8.95.

This work is characterized by its fine photography, good maps, authentic and interesting text. It is arranged basically to follow the books of the Bible and contains a complete index.

MAY, HERBERT G. *Oxford Bible atlas.* New York: Oxford University Press, 1962. Pp. 144. $4.95. Pap. $2.50.

This work contains four physical maps and 22 historical maps in chronological order. Every map is in five colors and is accompanied by a concise text. A 26-page gazetteer concludes the work.

*METZGER, BRUCE M. *The Oxford concise concordance to the Revised Standard Version of the Holy Bible.* New York: Oxford University Press, 1962. Pp. 158. $2.50.

This is not a complete concordance, but a compact, usable work containing those nouns, verbs, adjectives, adverbs, and proper names which will be of interest to the general reader.

MILLER, MADELINE S. and MILLER, J. L. *Harper's Bible dictionary.* 7th ed. New York: Harper, 1961. Pp. 854. $8.95.

The format of this work is one with two columns on a page. The entry on Jesus Christ is ten pages long, the one on Moses about three, but ordinarily there are two or three entries to a column. The work is amply illustrated, and maps are provided at the end of the book. As a late-comer to the field of Bible dictionaries, this work has eliminated some of the deficiencies of earlier dictionaries' efforts. A large group of Protestant scholars contributed to its production.

THOMPSON, NEWTON W. and STOCK, RAYMOND. *Complete concordance to the Bible* (Douay version). 4th ed. St. Louis: B. Herder Book Co., 1945. Pp. 1,914. $17.00.

Although this work may be superseded because of the obsolescence of the Douay version, it can be a useful intermediary tool for those familiar with the Douay texts.

WRIGHT, G. E. and FILSON, F. V. *The Westminster historical atlas to the Bible.* Rev. ed. Philadelphia: Westminster Press, 1956. Pp. 103. $7.50.

A standard work that has long been in the field and has been kept up-to-date. The text is perhaps the best of recent historical geographies.

THE ZONDERVAN PICTORIAL BIBLE DICTIONARY. Merritt C. Tenney, general editor. Grand Rapids: Zondervan Publishing House, 1963. Pp. 927. $9.95.

Done with the assistance of 65 contributing scholars and experts in various fields. It provides quick access to explanatory data and contains more than 5,000 entries and 40 pages of colored maps.

3. Introduction and Criticism

AHERN, BARNABAS, M., C.P. *New horizons in biblical theology.* Notre Dame, Ind.: Fides Publishers, 1964. Pp. 218. $3.95.

This single volume makes available to the average layman biblical studies which previously appeared in scholarly publications not generally available.

ALONSO SCHÖKEL, LUIS, S.J. *Understanding biblical research.* Translated by P.J. McCord, S.J. New York: Herder and Herder, 1963. Pp. 130. $3.50.

The author is a professor of OT exegesis at the Pontifical Biblical Institute in Rome. This book presents a modern scholar's approach to the study of the Bible.

BEGUIN, OLIVER. *Roman Catholicism and the Bible.* New York: Association Press, 1963. Pp. 95. Pap. $1.50.

The book considers the use of the Bible by Catholics in liturgy, catechetics, and mission fields. It contains a brief discussion of progressive and conservative elements among Catholic exegetes.

BOUYER, LOUIS, C. Or. *The meaning of Sacred Scripture.* Translated by Mary Perkins Ryan. Notre Dame, Ind.: University of Notre Dame Press, 1959. Pp. 259. $6.00. (Liturgical Studies, 5)

3

The author introduces the reader to both Old and New Testaments through a series of 22 short essays on biblical themes such as the covenant, the kingdom, Christian mystery, etc.

BRAUN, FRANCIS M., O.P. *The work of Père Lagrange.* Adapted from the French by R.T.A. Murphy, O.P. Milwaukee: Bruce, 1963. Pp. 306. $7.00.

An interesting biography of the famous Dominican exegete. In the final chapter the author traces the profound influence of Lagrange on modern Catholic biblical scholarship.

*BUTLER, BASIL CHRISTOPHER, O.S.B. *The Church and the Bible.* Baltimore, Md.: (Helicon) Taplinger, 1961. Pp. 111. $2.95.

In the three chapters which comprise this book, the author attempts to clarify the role of the Bible in its relation to the Church. In the first chapter he discusses the role of God's revelation in religion through the Incarnation; in the second, the relation between scripture and tradition, inspiration and the sources of revelation; and in the third, the central position of Christ in the Bible. The presentation is popular in character and eminently readable.

CHARLIER, CELESTIN, O.S.B. *The Christian approach to the Bible.* Translated by H. J. Richards and B. Peters. Westminster, Md.: Newman Press, 1958. Pp. 298. $4.00.

This volume has gone through several editions in the French original and is highly recommended by all reviewers. The author is a leader in the revival of interest in the Bible.

DANIEL-ROPS, HENRY. *What is the Bible?* Translated by J. R. Foster. New York: Hawthorn Books, 1958. Pp. 128. $3.50.

This inexpensive, valuable tool contains readable discussions of such topics as the origin and history of the Bible, its canon, inspiration, literary forms, historical value, etc.

FRAINE, JEAN DE, S.J. *The Bible and the origin of man.* New York: Desclee, 1962. Pp. x+85. $2.50.

This is an investigation of the hypothesis that all true men, past and present, have descended from a single couple. After investigating the scriptural texts which deal with evolution, the author concludes that such theological monogenism cannot be proved from the scriptures alone because the sacred author did not intend to pass judgment on the problem.

THE GOD OF ISRAEL, THE GOD OF CHRISTIANS; the great themes of Scripture. Translated by Kathryn Sullivan, R.S.C.J. New York: Desclee, 1961. Pp. vii+261. $3.95.

This collection of essays by distinguished authors is organized according to a five-fold structure: 1) God's plan, 2) God's revelation, 3) God's demands, 4) God's fidelity, 5) God's victory. The result is a sketch of a spirituality based on God's call and the response demanded by that call, the divine plan of salvation is unfolded in both testaments.

GOTTWALD, NORMAN K. *All the kingdoms of the earth.* New York: Harper and Row, 1964. Pp. $7.00.

The author analyzes scriptural texts which bear on history even down to the 20th century. He explores several prophetic themes and interprets political prophecies which give us a key biblical analysis for the present day.

GUILLET, JACQUES. *Themes of the Bible.* Translated by A. J. La Mothe, Jr. Notre Dame, Ind.: Fides, 1961. Pp. 279. $6.95.

The author examines significant theological terms such as grace, justice, truth, etc., from both the Old and New Testaments and describes the religious encounter reflected in these words. Each item aims to open new perspectives in salvation history.

HUNT, IGNATIUS, O.S.B. *Understanding the Bible.* New York: Sheed and Ward, 1962. Pp. 207. $3.95.

Using the results of the most recent scholarly research on the Bible, the author offers his readers a reappraisal of the sacred books in accord with recent papal directives.

JOHNSTON, LEONARD. *Witnesses to God.* New York: Sheed and Ward, 1961. Pp. 174. $3.50.

A brief, unified survey of the Bible as the word of God in act, bearing witness to himself through the great deeds recorded in Scripture, and finally in the Word made flesh.

JONES, ALEXANDER. *God's living Word.* New York: Sheed and Ward, 1961. Pp. 214. $3.95.

It is the author's chief concern to demonstrate the vitality of the word of God. In doing so he covers the whole range of biblical history and some of the difficult problems in that history. His analysis is penetrating and his expression is clear. The reader scarcely notices that he is reading about such difficult matters because the reading is so pleasurable.

LEVIE, JEAN, S.J. *The Bible: Word of God in words of men.* Translated by S. H. Treman. New York: P. J. Kenedy, 1962. Pp. 323. $7.50.

This is a critical exposition of the divine and human aspects of revelation. Although there are copious notes and bibliographical data, its approach is essentially to the educated layman. An excellent history of exegesis, both Catholic and Protestant, is presented.

McKENZIE, JOHN L., S.J. *Myths and realities:* Studies in biblical theology. Milwaukee: Bruce, 1963. Pp. xvi+285. $4.75.

This is a collection of the author's writings which have appeared in various scholarly journals over the past 10 years. As such the intended audience varies, but it is generally true to say that all the articles presuppose a certain familiarity with the subjects treated, on the part of the reader. The thought content of these essays range from subjects like intellectual liberty and inspiration to myth and messianism. The author's thesis that inspiration as a charism belongs to the religious community, with the writer being only a spokesman for the community, has caught the attention of many scholars.

MORAN, G., F.S.C. *Scripture and tradition:* a survey of the controversy. New York: Herder and Herder, 1963. Pp. 127. $2.95.

Recent ecumenical concern and the Second Vatican Council have heightened interest in the subject of this book, which is clearly indicated by the title. The author presents both sides of the question and then suggests possible avenues of agreement.

MOWINCKEL, SIGMUND OLAF PLYTT. *The Old Testament as word of God.* Translated by R. B. Bjurnard. New York: Abingdon Press, 1959. Pp. 144. $2.75.

The author aims at making the OT come alive for the reader. He emphasizes the dynamic activity of the word of God as the entire activity of God.

PRICE, IRA M., and others. *The monuments and the Old Testament;* light from the Near East on the Scriptures. Rev. ed. Philadelphia: Judson Press, 1959. Pp. 450. $6.75.

The author is professor of Semitic languages and literature at the University of Chicago. His work has stood the test of time and has been brought up-to-date with the most recent archeological finds and biblical scholarship.

RAHNER, KARL, S.J. *Inspiration in the Bible.* Translated by C. H. Henkey. New York: Herder and Herder, 1961. Pp. 80. Pap. $1.95. (Quaestiones Disputatae, 1)

Rahner insists on the uniqueness of the apostolic age and its connection with the Scriptures. In effect he weds the oral tradition of the primitive Church with the written word to support his thesis that God's will is the inspiring originator of the sacred texts.

SOCIETY FOR OLD TESTAMENT STUDY. *Documents from Old Testament times.* Edited by D. W. Thomas. New York: Nelson, 1958. Pp. 302. $5.00. Pap. $1.75.

Like Pritchard's work on ancient Near East texts, this is a collection of documents that relate to OT times. The texts have been translated and provided with introductions by members of the Society.

4. Commentaries and Exegesis on the Whole Bible

A CATHOLIC COMMENTARY ON HOLY SCRIPTURE. Edited by Bernard Orchard, E. F. Sutcliffe, R. C. Fuller, and R. Russell. New York: Nelson, 1953. Pp. 1,296. $15.00.

While the tone of the work definitely tends toward the conservative, and should be brought up to date, it is the only one-volume, complete Catholic commentary available.

PEAKE'S COMMENTARY ON THE BIBLE. Edited by M. Black and H. H. Rowley. New York: Nelson, 1962. Pp. 1,126. $15.00.

The Protestant counterpart to the work immediately above, in arrangement and format. However, this work is superior in its quality of scholarship. It is designed to place before the reader in simple form the generally accepted results of biblical criticism, interpretation, history and theology.

THE TWENTIETH CENTURY BIBLE COMMENTARY. Edited by G. H. Davies. Rev. ed. New York: Harper, 1955. Pp. 571. $6.95.

A one-volume commentary compiled from the contributions of reputable Protestant scholars. There are some very good introductory chapters and these are followed by a phrase by phrase commentary on the books taken in order.

B. OLD TESTAMENT

1. Early Backgrounds, Archeology and Antiquities

ALBRIGHT, WILLIAM FOXWELL. *Archeology and the religion of Israel.* 4th ed. Baltimore: Johns Hopkins Press, 1956. Pp. 246. $5.00.

The archeological and historical background of the premonarchic and monarchic religion of Israel is elucidated in this book.

————. *The archeology of Palestine.* Rev. ed. New York: Peter Smith, 1960. Pp. 271. $3.00. Pap. Pelican (A199) $1.25.

A survey of archeological technique and excavation in Palestine; arranged by periods from the Old Stone Age to NT times.

_____ . *The biblical period from Abraham to Ezra.* New York: Harper, 1952. Pp. 120 Pap. Torchbooks (Tb102) $1.35.

This study traces the history of Israel from the Mosaic period to the restoration. It is detailed and imparts much information.

_____ . *From the Stone Age to Christianity.* 2d ed. with a new introduction. Baltimore, Md.: Johns Hopkins Press, 1957. Pp. 423. $5.00. Pap. Anchor (A100) $1.45.

The new introduction which the author has written for this book is a classic in its own right. He asserts that recent archeological discoveries have left his views fundamentally unchanged. He comments on such biblical concepts as monotheism, the covenant, and prophecy. In his second chapter which was rewritten he disagrees with the philosophy of history entertained by Arnold Toynbee and deplores the latter's prejudiced attacks on ancient Israel and its historical role.

THE BIBLE AND THE ANCIENT NEAR EAST; essays in honor of William Foxwell Albright. Edited by G. E. Wright. Garden City, N.Y.: Doubleday, 1961. Pp. 409. $7.50.

This is an Albright *festschrift* containing 14 essays covering a broad spectrum of OT background subjects. Many of the experts who contributed are Albright's former students.

*BURROWS, MILLAR. *What mean these stones?* The significance of archeology for biblical studies. New York: Meridian Books, 1957. Pp. 306. $1.35.

Published originally by the American School of Oriental Research in 1941. It comes from the author's conviction that much of what has been written on archeology and the Bible has missed the mark. He attempts to put the whole matter in its true light. The first chapter is an introduction to archeology. Following chapters discuss texts and languages, topography and chronology, material and secular backgrounds, religious and ethical backgrounds and finally archeologists' explanations, illustrations and evaluations.

FINEGAN, JACK. *Light from the Ancient past.* 2d ed. Princeton: Princeton University Press, 1959. Pp. 638. $10.00.

The fact that the first edition of this book went through six printings is a witness to its popularity as a reliable survey. This new edition takes into account the material revealed by the Qumrân discoveries and is 138 pages longer than the first. There are 204 illustrations which are generally good. The chief merits of this work are completeness and dependability in its judgments.

GLUECK, NELSON. *The other side of the Jordan.* New Haven: American Schools of Oriental Research, 1940. Pp. 208. Unbound, Stechert, $1.00.

The opening chapter of this well-written and profusely illustrated book is a general essay on biblical archeology. The remaining five chapters describe some of the author's Transjordanian excavations.

_____ . *Rivers in the desert.* New York: Grove, 1960. Pp. 302. Pap. Evergreen (E206) $3.95.

Based on the author's six years of work in the Negev, this book visually describes the civilizations which once flourished there.

GRAY, JOHN. *Archeology and the Old Testament world.* New York: Nelson, 1962. Pp. 256. $6.50.

To undertake the publication of a book on such a vast subject required a great deal of work and courage on the part of the author. What is perhaps even more astounding is his success in presenting the fruits of his research in a form that is so eminently readable. The author concentrates especially on ancient Middle Eastern manuscripts and their affinity to the OT.

*HARDING, GEORGE LANCASTER. *The antiquities of Jordan.* New York: Crowell, 1960. Pp. 206. $4.75.

The author was in charge of Jordan's Department of Antiquities for over 20 years. A general introduction treating the history, topography, climate, and inhabitants is followed by a description of archeological finds at Jarash, Petra and Jericho, and the discovery of the Dead Sea Scrolls.

KENYON, KATHLEEN. *Archeology in the Holy Land.* New York: Frederick A. Praeger, 1960. Pp. 326. $7.50. Pap. $3.45.

This brings up to date Albright's classical work on the subject. It is of interest to both the general reader and the more serious student.

_____. *Beginning in archeology.* Rev. ed. New York: Frederick A. Praeger, 1953. Pp. 220. $5.00. Pap. $2.45.

The purpose of this book is to orientate beginners in archeological field work, rendering more intelligible the practical experience that should be acquired in actual excavation. It has been judged as a very successful attempt to describe the actual technique of modern excavations. Therefore, this little volume will prove of interest to the beginner in archeology and will give the student of biblical theology a better understanding of archeology as it relates to his studies.

*NOTH, MARTIN. *The history of Israel.* 2d ed. New translation by G. B. F. Brandon. New York: Harper, 1960. Pp. 487. $6.00.

Some uncomplimentary things were said about this book when it first appeared in English. The fault, however, lay with the defective translation. In its new form we have an accurate presentation of the original, and the overall effect is a usable and reliable book for students of the OT.

PRITCHARD, JAMES BENNET. *Archeology and the Old Testament.* Princeton, N.J.: Princeton University Press, 1958. Pp. 263. $5.00.

An appraisal of how our knowledge of the written history of the Hebrew Bible has been modified and enlarged by archeology. The book is in non-technical language and artistically illustrated.

THOMPSON, J. A. *The Bible and archeology.* Grand Rapids, Mich.: Eerdmans, 1962. Pp. 467. $5.95.

This volume contains three titles formerly published separately: *Archeology and the Old Testament, Archeology and the Pre-Christian Centuries,* and *Archeology in the New Testament.* It is intended for general readers.

2. Introduction and Criticism

ANDERSON, BERNHARD W. *Understanding the Old Testament.* Englewood Cliffs, N.J.: Prentice-Hall, 1957. Pp. xxiii+521. $7.95.

Beginning with the Exodus, the author delineates the development of Israel as a community, the People of God. In the process he highlights the relationship of God with his people and the increasing awareness of their calling and their obligations. He emphasizes the importance of understanding the history of Israel through understanding her faith.

BRIGHT, JOHN. *A history of Israel.* Philadelphia: Westminster Press, 1959. Pp. 500. $7.50.

The author, a former student of W. F. Albright at Johns Hopkins, here presents the first systematic history that incorporates the views of his mentor. Bright presumes that the reader has some background information. He presents Israel in its geographical and chronological context and shows that her written narratives conformed to the much earlier events which they narrate.

CORNFELD, GAALYAHU. *From Daniel to Paul.* New York: Macmillan, 1962. Pp. 376. $13.95.

Among the various subjects portrayed in this book are the Jewish conflict with Graeco-Roman civilization, the historical and religious background to the Hasmoneans, the Dead Sea Scrolls, the NT world, and the Bar-Kochba war.

DANIÉLOU, JEAN, S.J. *From shadows to reality:* studies in the biblical typology of the Fathers. Translated by W. Hibbard. Westminster, Md.: Newman, 1961. Pp. 296. $5.50.

This book attempts to establish links between the typological exegesis of the NT and the great doctors of the fourth century. The author's final conclusion is that typology is an integral part of the deposit of revelation.

DRIVER, SAMUEL R. *An introduction to the literature of the Old Testament.* 9th ed. New York: Peter Smith, 1962. Pp. 577. $4.25, pap. Meridian (MG29) $2.75.

This book was first published in 1891, but in spite of its age it is still basic.

ELLIS, PETER F., C.SS.R. *The men and the message of the Old Testament.* Collegeville, Minn.: Liturgical Press, 1963. Pp. xxiv+559. $8.00. Pap. $3.95.

This work is directed to three distinct groups of readers: college students, those whose studies are ancillary to the study of sacred theology, and those who recite the Divine Office. The three are separate and distinct, but integrated by the author's treatment of each part with an introduction, a literary analysis, and a study of psalms. This book encourages the reader to go to the OT text, and makes its reading intelligible. It presents scholars' new approach whose course was set by biblical archeologists and by Pius XII.

GOTTWALD, NORMAN K. *A light to the nations;* an introduction to the Old Testament. New York: Harper, 1959. Pp. 615. $6.95.

A suitable text of OT studies for use in a college survey course. The author covers the history of Israel from the patriarchs to Qumrân. In preliminary chapters he treats such concepts as literary form, canon, texts, and versions, and historical and geographical background. Unfortunately he has overlooked and misrepresented Catholic scholarship. Therefore, while it would not be suitable for the Catholic classroom, Catholic scholars could use it as a model for its completeness, its order and clarity, and its attractive style.

HARRELSON, WALTER. *Interpreting the Old Testament.* New York: Holt, Rinehart and Winston, 1964. Pp. xi+529. $9.95, text ed. $7.50.

The OT books are treated in the order of the English Bible. The author, a non-Catholic, provides a special introduction to each book. The scholarship is sound, the presentation fresh.

9

MORIARTY, FREDERICK L. *Introducing the Old Testament.* Milwaukee: Bruce, 1960. Pp. 253. $4.25.

This introduction approaches the subject through 15 biographies of OT characters, ranging from Abraham to Daniel.

PRITCHARD, JAMES BENNET, ed. *The ancient Near East;* an anthology of texts and pictures. Princeton, N.J.: Princeton University Press, 1958. Pp. 280. $7.50.

This work is an effective synthesis of two former works by the author, one on texts and one on pictures. It is a useful, scholarly work, and within the economic range of most students.

*ROWLEY, HAROLD H. *The re-discovery of the Old Testament.* Philadelphia: Westminster Press, 1946. Pp. 314. $3.00.

Against a background of archeology and history, the distinguished scripture scholar focuses on the wider context of the OT. His purpose, however, is not to record and clarify secular history, but to help the reader to a fuller apprehension of the religious meaning of the scriptures.

TOS, ALDO J. *Approaches to the Bible: The Old Testament.* Englewood Cliffs, N.J.: Prentice-Hall, 1963. Pp. 286. Pap. $5.25.

This work systematically traces the theme of salvation history in order to counteract the frequent impression of a lack of continuity and unity in the OT. The author compresses much information into a short book. It is scholarly, up-to-date, and easy to read.

VAUX, ROLAND DE, O.P. *Ancient Israel.* Translated by J. McHugh. New York: McGraw-Hill, 1961. Pp. 592. $10.95.

The author makes the results of his own critical research and experience available to the non-specialist, and thus seeks to impart to him the basis for a more intelligent reading of the Bible. The scope of the work embraces practically all of the customs and cultural institutions of the People of Israel.

3. Commentaries and Exegesis on the Whole Old Testament

OLD TESTAMENT READING GUIDE. Edited by W. Heidt, O.S.B., C. Stuhlmueller, C.P., K. Sullivan, R.S.C.J., and B. M. Ahern, C.P. 30 parts. Collegeville, Minn.: Liturgical Press, 1965. Pap. $0.40 each. In progress.

Like its counterpart for the NT, this series presents the latest and soundest biblical scholarship in a brief, clear, and attractive way. The experts who are contributing to this series are addressing themselves to the educated layman. The text used is that of the Confraternity of Christian Doctrine.

PAMPHLET BIBLE SERIES. Edited by J. J. McEleneny, C.S.P. New York: Paulist Press, 1959. Pap. $0.75 each.

Still in progress, each pamphlet is about 100 pages in length and is devoted to a specific book of the Bible. The contributors have been selected from among the experts in Catholic scripture studies. The text used in the commentary is that of the Confraternity of Christian Doctrine.

SIMONS, J. J. *The geographical and topographical texts of the Old Testament;* a concise commentary in thirty-two chapters. Leiden: E. J. Brill, 1959. Pp. 613. $30.00.

As one might expect from the size of this volume, it is not meant to be read through continuously. Indeed it is not intended for neophytes, but as a vademecum for serious students. By the analysis and interpretation of geographical and topographical texts of the OT it solves many of the problems encountered in reading these passages. Its commentaries are not exhaustive.

4. Commentaries on Individual Parts of the Old Testament
a) Pentateuch

BONHOEFFER, DIETRICH. *Creation and fall;* a theological interpretation of Genesis 1-3. Translated by J. C. Fletcher. New York: Macmillan, 1959. Pp. 96. Pap. $1.50.

The author is thoroughly convinced that the OT is fulfilled in the New, and that the Church only sees the beginning in the end. His method is scientific, yet his style is very readable.

NOTH, MARTIN. *Exodus;* a commentary. Translated by J. S. Bowden. Philadelphia: Westminster Press, 1962. Pp. 284. $5.00. (Old Testament library)

Almost the entire book is devoted to commentary. The author's extremely critical approach reflects his competence in this difficult field, and yet he expresses himself in terms which can be understood by the average intelligent layman.

NORTH, ROBERT G. *Sociology of the Biblical Jubilee.* Rome: Pontifical Biblical Institute, 1954. Pp. 245. $6.25.

Published for scholars and replete with critical apparatus, this work is not easy reading. But when read through it enables the reader to well understand the nature of the biblical jubilee.

RAD, GERARD VON. *Genesis:* a commentary. Translated by J. H. Marks. Philadelphia: Westminster Press, 1964. Pp. 434. $7.50.

This excellent book elucidates the relationship between biblical, historical, and literary criticism, vis-à-vis a biblical theology of history. The text, when not differing from the author's own translation, is from the R.S.V.

RENCKENS, HENRICUS, S.J. *Israel's concept of the beginning;* the theology of Genesis 1-3. New York: Herder and Herder, 1964. Pp. 320. $5.95.

This is the story of the creation of the first man and of the fall, as these were understood by the people of Israel and as they must be understood by Christians of our age. It is a modern investigation of the text in the light of its primitive literary form. It is not a verse by verse commentary, but a consideration of various themes.

ROUTLEY, ERIK. *Beginning the Old Testament;* studies in Genesis and Exodus for the general reader. Philadelphia: Fortress Press, 1962. Pp. 159. $2.50.

This non-technical study effectively presents a general view based on current biblical studies.

ROWLEY, HAROLD H. *From Joseph to Joshua;* biblical traditions in the light of archeology. New York: Oxford University Press, 1950. Pp. 200. $4.15.

Although somewhat dated, this work serves to familiarize readers with Pentateuchal literature. Not all scholars agree with the author's conclusions, but scholars themselves have not reached a consensus on the dynamic problems discussed by the author.

SUELZER, ALEXA, S.P. *The Pentateuch;* a study in salvation history. New York: Herder and Herder, 1964. Pp. 224. $4.75.

This popularization clarifies the origin, scope, and main themes of the Pentateuch. It supersedes most other popularizations on the same subject.

VAWTER, Bruce, C.M. *A path through Genesis.* New York: Sheed and Ward, 1956. Pp. 308. $4.00.

Highly recommended, this book helps to solve some of the difficulties which the educated Catholic layman has encountered in reading Genesis. It can provide background for understanding the encyclical *Humani Generis.*

b) Historical Books

SULLIVAN, KATHRYN, R.S.C.J. *God's word and work;* the message of the Old Testament historical books. Collegeville, Minn.: Liturgical Press, 1958. Pp. 164. $3.00.

This is a collection of articles which appeared in *Worship.* Mother Sullivan recreates the great redemptive acts of God towards Israel. Scripture is seen as an integral part of Christian life.

c) Prophetic Literature

BOUTFLOWER, CHARLES. *In and around the Book of Daniel.* Grand Rapids, Mich.: Zondervan Publishing House, 1963. Pp. xviii+312. $4.95.

These are well-reasoned and instructive pages which throw considerable light on an interesting but difficult section of Sacred Scripture. The historical difficulties are plentiful, but the author discusses them and presents the information which the reader needs to decide the questions for himself.

*CHAINE, JOSEPH. *God's heralds;* a guide to the prophets of Israel. Translated by B. McGrath, O.S.B. New York: Joseph Wagner, 1953. Pp. 336. $3.95.

The author was a layman but professor of Sacred Scripture at Lyons for 27 years. Here he gives sufficient information about OT figures to make reading their prophecies more interesting and more intelligible. This book does not give a phrase by phrase commentary on the prophets, but it gives the reader a clear idea of their mission and message.

HESCHEL, ABRAHAM J. *The prophets.* New York: Harper, 1962. Pp. xix+518. $6.00.

This book provides new insights to stimulate further thinking on this subject. The main goal of the author is to analyze the significance of prophecy in the history of religion, and the nature of prophetic inspiration.

*KISSANE, EDWARD J. *The Book of Isaiah.* 2v. Dublin: Browne and Nolan, 1941-43. $4.50 each.

A work which is fully scientific. The author is thorough and accurate in his treatment of details. To his scholarliness there is united a sustained and well-poised view of the wider context of his subject. The overall result is contribution toward the understanding of a difficult portion of the Bible.

LESLIE, ELMER A. *Isaiah.* New York: Abingdon Press, 1963. Pp. 288. $5.00.

The aim of this work is to make the reading of Isaiah an informative and inspiring experience. One of the most distinguishing features of the book is the arrangement of all 66 chapters of Isaiah in chronological order.

MORGAN, G. CAMPBELL. *The minor prophets;* the men and their messages. Westwood, N.J.: Revell, 1960. Pp. 157. $3.25.

This work grew out of a series of lectures delivered some years ago. The Protestant author has emphasized the tenderness of God's love. First he gives the text, then a special introduction, followed by a brief commentary.

ROWLEY, HAROLD H. *Men of God;* studies in Old Testament history and prophecy. New York: Nelson, 1963. Pp. 306. $8.50.

A collection of lectures originally delivered at John Rylands Library in Manchester. Each is a survey of various views that have been advanced in relation to outstanding biblical characters like Moses, Elijah, Hosea, Hezekiah, Jeremiah, Ezekiel and Nehemiah. The author admittedly disagrees with some scholars, but he has not succeeded to align their views to his own either.

STUHLMUELLER, CARROLL, C.P. *The prophets and the word of God.* Notre Dame, Ind.: Fides Publishers, 1964. Pp. 324. $4.95.

Except for one chapter, this book is a collection of articles previously published by the author in various periodicals. It is a biblical popularization for the educated layman. With the word of God being the unifying theme and not much more which might make for a greater continuity between chapters, one could hardly consider this to be a complete introduction to the prophetic writers of the OT. Many things are omitted, but if the book is judged according to the modern literary form of "collected reprints" it will be understood as a contribution to the deeper understanding of the prophets.

VAWTER, BRUCE, C.M. *The conscience of Israel;* Pre-exilic prophets and prophecy. New York: Sheed and Ward, 1961. Pp. 308. $5.00.

Often the neophyte is inclined to see the prophets too much in the light of the NT. Father Vawter reminds the reader that although the OT was a preparation for the NT, the prophets were Israelites, men of their times. He therefore seeks to promote an understanding of the prophets by sketching the historical milieu in which they lived.

d) Wisdom Literature

GASNIER, MICHAEL, O.P. *The Psalms, school of spirituality.* Translated by Dom Aldhelm Dean. St. Louis: B. Herder Book Co., 1962. Pp. v+160. $3.75.

Unfortunately the translator used the Douay Version for the psalms. Otherwise the book is helpful in putting the psalms in their proper settings and in delineating the theological themes found in them.

HIMEBAUGH, CECILIA, SISTER, O.S.B. *The psalms in modern life.* Chicago: H. Regnery Co., 1960. Pp. 259. $4.50.

Fifty well-known psalms, arranged and explained so that they become immediate to the situation and needs of modern Christians.

JONES, EDGAR. *Proverbs and Ecclesiastes;* introduction and commentary. New York: Macmillan, 1961. Pp. 349. $4.25. (Torch Bible Commentaries.)

The arrangement of this work is a verse by verse commentary on each of the books, with a valuable special introduction preceding the commentary.

*KISSANE, EDWARD J. *The Book of Job.* New York: Sheed and Ward, 1946. Pp. xliv+298. $4.00.

An excellent, widely-acclaimed volume. The passage of time has in no way devaluated this work. The author, an established exegete, gives an introduction to Job, followed by a translation and a compact commentary.

* _____ . *Book of Psalms.* 2v. New York: Newman Press, 1953. $10.00 set.

This work on the psalms is characterized by the same precision and lucidity for which the author has become known.

LAMBERT, W. G. *Babylonian wisdom literature.* New York: Oxford University Press, 1960. Pp. xviii+358, 75 plates. $16.00.

This is a monumental work of transcribed texts, transliterations and annotated translations by the head of the department of Semetic studies at Johns Hopkins University. It, like the works of Pritchard, offers the biblical student comparative background for understanding the writings of the OT in the same genre.

MURPHY, ROLAND E., O. Carm. *Seven Books of Wisdom.* Milwaukee: Bruce, 1960. Pp. 163. $3.75.

The editor of *Catholic Biblical Quarterly* and professor of OT studies at Catholic University has here presented a worthy introduction to the wisdom of Israel. This is the best companion to Wisdom literature available in English. The analysis is thoroughly up-to-date. The author, however, rarely makes any definitive judgments on controversial questions.

*SOCIETY FOR OLD TESTAMENT STUDY. *Wisdom in Israel and in the ancient Near East.* Leiden: E. J. Brill, 1955. Pp. 301. $8.75.

This *festschrift* was presented to Professor Rowley by the Society in association with the editorial board of *Vetus Testamentum,* in celebration of his sixty-fifth birthday. It contains 22 essays by such notables as Albright, Driver, Ginsberg and von Rad.

WEISER, ARTHUR. *The Psalms;* a commentary. 4th ed. Philadelphia: Westminster Press, 1962. Pp. 841. $9.50.

A professor at Tübingen since 1930, the author is a distinguished scholar. This is one of the most exhaustive works ever published on the psalms. It is divided into two parts: the first is a detailed introduction; the second, the text, based on the R.S.V., followed by commentary on the individual psalms.

5. Old Testament Theology

BEAUCAMP, EVODE, O.F.M. *The Bible and the universe;* Israel and the theology of history. Translated by D. Balhatchet. Westminster, Md.: Newman, 1963. Pp. 200. $4.75.

The author attempts to answer the question: what is the role of the universe in the drama of salvation? His approach is different from that of Teilhard de Chardin, but also very interesting and instructive.

DENTAN, ROBERT C. *Preface to Old Testament theology.* Rev. ed. New York: Seabury Press, 1963. Pp. 146. $3.00.

An inquiry into the character and method of OT theology. The author suggests that the Thomistic outline of systematic theology is still the best.

HEINISCH, PAUL. *Theology of the Old Testament.* Translated by W. Heidt. Collegeville, Minn.: Liturgical Press, 1950. Pp. 386. $4.00. Pap. $1.95.

The author was one of the foremost biblical scholars in the world. The 6,000 scriptural references attest to the fact that he has spared no pains in gathering texts which pertain to revealed truth. In a familiar Thomistic outline, this work constitutes the only full length, exhaustive, systematic presentation of Old Testament theology.

JACOB, EDMUND. *Theology of the Old Testament.* Translated by A. W. Heathcote and P. J. Allcock. New York: Harper, 1958. Pp. 368. $5.00.

This is a summary of the recent advances in the theology of the OT. It brings the reader up to date on matters that affect his understanding of the Bible. A fine book for the student, priest, and educated layman.

McKENZIE, JOHN L., S.J. *The two-edged sword.* Milwaukee: Bruce, 1956. Pp. 317. $4.50.

This book is not the communication of one scholar to another, but rather an attempt at solid popularization. The author has successfully treated every major theme of OT theology. He does not answer every difficulty that presents itself, but the reader can experience the sweep and the power of the sacred books, the hope which brightens their pages, and the incomprehensible love of God for man.

SALM, CELESTINE LUKE, ed. *Studies in salvation history.* Englewood Cliffs, N.J.: Prentice-Hall, 1964. Pp. xvii+236. Pap. $2.95.

The purpose of this collection is to bring to light articles previously published in journals and proceedings not easily available to the general public. Articles were selected for the interested, educated non-specialist. All articles reflect the best of contemporary American biblical scholarship.

RAD, GERHARD VON. *Old Testament theology;* the theology of Israel's historical traditions. Translated by D. M. G. Stalker, New York: Harper, 1962. Pp. 483. $8.00.

The theological part of this book is preceded by a short section on history. Throughout, depth of scholarship and wisdom are coupled with freshness of style.

*SUTCLIFFE, EDMUND F., S.J. *Providence and suffering in the Old and New Testaments.* New York: Nelson, 1953. Pp. 175.

Nine chapters of this book are devoted to pre-Christian development of the concept of suffering. Finally, in the tenth chapter the author recapitulates and shows the transcendence of the NT.

VRIEZEN, THEODORE. *An outline of Old Testament theology.* Translated by S. Neuijen. Newton Centre, Mass.: Charles T. Branford Co., 1958. Pp. 388. $7.50.

This translation was made from the second revised edition of the original Dutch. The book contains two parts: I. An introduction to the OT which considers such things as the relationship between the OT and the Church. II. The content of OT theology, which considers the nature of God, the nature of man, and the relationship between the two as known from the OT.

WRIGHT, GEORGE ERNEST. *God who acts.* Naperville, Ill.: Allenson, 1958. Pp. 132. Pap. $2.25.

The author outlines the great acts of God in salvation history. For the non-specialist this will serve as a summary of all that archeology and other modern scientific disciplines have taught us with respect to the interpretation of the scriptures.

_____. *The Old Testament against its environment.* Naperville, Ill.: Allenson, 1958. Pp. 115. $2.00.

A highly recommended work. It gives the nature of Israelite religion in contrast to that of surrounding nations.

C. THE INTERTESTAMENTAL PERIOD

1. Early Background of the New Testament

BARRETT, CHARLES K. *The New Testament background:* selected documents. New York: Seabury Press, 1956. Pp. 276. $4.50. Pap. Torchbks. (TB86) $1.65.

This book contains more than 200 documents in translation. They range over the more significant aspects of the cultural milieu into which Christianity came.

FARMER, WILLIAM R. *Maccabees, Zealots, and Josephus:* an inquiry into Jewish nationalism in the Graeco-Roman period. New York: Columbia University Press, 1956. Pp. 239. $4.50.

This book supplies information for the intertestamental period on the subject indicated in the subtitle, which is treated only obliquely in the scriptures themselves.

FOERSTER, WERNER. *From the Exile to Christ;* a historical introduction to Palestinian Judaism. Translated by G. E. Harris. Philadelphia: Fortress Press, 1964. Pp. xiv+247. $4.85.

This survey outlines the periods from the Exile through the fall of Jerusalem. There is an extended analysis of the social and cultural situation of Palestine at the time of Christ. Finally, the author concentrates on the religious factors prevalent at the time, especially Pharisaism.

PFEIFFER, ROBERT HENRY. *History of New Testament times:* with an introduction to the Apocrypha. New York: Harper, 1949. Pp. 561. $5.00.

Not exactly NT as the title would imply, but more the intertestamental period. A useful work for the statement of problems and the survey of opinions.

RUSSELL, DAVID S. *Between the Testaments.* Philadelphia: Fortress Press, 1960. Pp. 176. $2.50.

A short review of cultural, historical and literary backgrounds which preceded the time of Christ, with some emphasis given to the Essenes.

TCHERIKOVER, AVIGDOR. *Hellenistic civilization and the Jews.* Translated by S. Applebaum. Philadelphia: Jewish Publication Society of America, 1959. Pp. 566. $6.00.

This scholarly presentation covers the history of the Jews between the conquest of Alexander and the Roman period.

2. New Testament Archeology

GUARDUCCI, MARGHERITA. *The tomb of St. Peter;* the new discoveries in the sacred grottoes of the Vatican. Translated by J. McLellan. New York: Hawthorn, 1960. Pp. 200. $4.95.

A popular study of the Vatican grafiti presented with thoroughness.

ILLUSTRATED NEW TESTAMENT. Collegeville, Minn.: Liturgical Press, 1964. Pp. 256. $3.00. Pap. $1.00.

Basically this is a presentation of the NT in the Confraternity translation. On every page there are several pictures apropos to the text found on the same page. This provides an excellent visual aid for the reader and constitutes a course in history and archeology.

KIRSCHBAUM, ENGELBERT, S.J. *The tombs of St. Peter and St. Paul.* Translated by J. Murray, S.J. New York: St. Martin's Press, 1959. Pp. 247. $7.50.

As professor of archeology at the Gregorianum in Rome, the author was one of the four who made the official report on the excavations in question. This is a translation of an account published in German for the general reader. It is well illustrated.

KOPP, CLEMENS. *The holy places of the Gospels.* Translated by R. Walls. New York: Herder and Herder, 1963. Pp. xvii+424. $8.50.

This book is arranged chronologically according to the life of Jesus. It is critical and free from bias, a scholarly, documented work based on the author's long residence in the Holy Land. Many years were devoted to its preparation.

WEISER, FRANCIS, S.J. *The Holy Land;* a pilgrim's description in word and picture. Collegeville, Minn.: Liturgical Press, 1965. Pp. viii+184. $4.00.

This volume relates the author's journey to the Holy Land. As such it is an easily readable source of information on biblical geography and history of those 5 countries which can claim the honor of having witnessed the physical presence of our Lord. It will be a helpful background study for students in Bible courses and inspirational reading for those interested in the life of Christ and in the history of salvation. The text is enhanced with 16 pages of colored photos and many in black and white.

3. The Dead Sea Scrolls and the Qumrân Community

BLACK, MATTHEW. *The scrolls and Christian origins:* studies in the Jewish background of the New Testament. New York: Scribner's, 1961. Pp. 206. $3.95.

This attempt to determine the influence of the Essenes on Christianity depicts Qumrân as the direct source of Christianity.

BROWNLEE, WILLIAM HUGH. *The meaning of the Qumrân scrolls for the Bible,* with special attention to the Book of Isaiah. New York: Oxford University Press, 1964. Pp. 309. $7.50.

This examination of the Dead Sea texts emphasizes their significance for textual criticism of the Old Testament. The author believes that the Scrolls, far from detracting from the significance of the Gospel, enrich and reinforce that significance for the Christian.

BURROWS, MILLAR. *The Dead Sea Scrolls,* with translations by the author. New York: Viking, 1955. Pp. 435. $6.50.

_____. *More light on the Dead Sea Scrolls;* new scrolls and new interpretations, with translations of important recent discoveries. New York: Viking, 1958. Pp. 434. $6.50.

This work and the preceding one by the same author, give a view of some of the problems raised by the Scrolls. Both afford a good introduction to the subject for anyone who wishes to do serious study.

CARMIGNAC, JEAN. *Christ and the Teacher of Righteousness:* the evidence of the Dead Sea Scrolls. Translated by K. G. Pedley. Baltimore: (Helicon) Taplinger, 1962. Pp. 168. $3.95.

The author concludes that there are parallels between the Essenes and early Christianity, but that the Teacher of Righteousness is not depicted as the Messiah, as divine, or as crucified. W. F. Albright has written the preface.

CROSS, FRANK M., Jr. *The ancient library of Qumrân and modern biblical studies.* Garden City, N.Y.: Doubleday, 1958. Pp. 196. $4.50, abridged ed. pap. (A272) $1.25.

This outstanding work grew out of the Haskell Lectures which were delivered to the graduate school of theology at Oberlin College. It presupposes an elementary knowledge of the Scrolls and presents a well-rounded picture of the community responsible for them.

DANIELOU, JEAN, S. J. *The Dead Sea Scrolls and primitive Christianity.* Translated by S. Attanasio. Baltimore: (Helicon) Taplinger, 1959. Pp. 128. $3.00. Pap. Mentor Omega books (MP405) $0.60.

This is a familiar study of the resemblances and contrasts between the doctrine of the Scrolls and Christianity. It is useful, but because of its brevity tends toward oversimplification.

MILIK, JOZEF T. *Ten years of discovery in the wilderness of Judaea.* Naperville, Ill.: Allenson, 1959. Pp. 160. Pap. $2.85.

One of the best syntheses on the Scrolls that has appeared in any language, written by a man who has been involved with them from their first discovery. The presentation is on a popular level, but because it presupposes a certain familiarity with the subject it may not be the best book with which to begin a study of the Scrolls.

*PLOEG, JAN P. VAN DER. *The excavations at Qumrân:* a survey of the Judean brotherhood and its ideas. Translated by K. Smyth. London: Longmans, Green, 1958. Pp. 233. $4.00.

A thorough account of the story of the Dead Sea Scrolls, which bears the touch of a master and goes into every major issue raised by the discovery of the Scrolls. The author was eminently competent to produce such a work for he is an outstanding biblical scholar, the first to identify any of the Scrolls and the first to translate any of them into a modern language. His judgments and observations are marked by a constant maturity and accuracy, and his presentation is very simple.

SUTCLIFFE, EDMUND F., S. J. *The monks of Qumrân as depicted in the Dead Sea Scrolls.* With translations in English. Westminster, Md.: Newman Press, 1960. Pp. 272. $5.50.

The subject is treated in two parts: first, the site, buildings, economy and doctrines of the community are described; then the author's translations of texts bearing on these beliefs and the way of life of the group are given.

*VERMES, GAZA. *The Dead Sea Scrolls in English.* New York: Peter Smith, 1962. Pp. 255. $3.25. Pap. Pelican (A551) $1.25.

This is a reasonably priced English translation of the Scrolls with a 68-page introduction on the community responsible for them.

*_____. *Discovery in the Judean Desert.* New York: Desclee, 1956. Pp. 237. $5.00.

A good survey of the early phases of discovery and work on the Qumrân Scrolls.

D. NEW TESTAMENT

1. English Versions

KLEIST, JAMES A. and LILLY, JOSEPH L. *The New Testament* rendered from the original Greek with explanatory notes. Milwaukee: Bruce, 1954. $6.00; text edition, $4.20.

A translation from the Greek text of Bover into accurate, current, American English. The translation of the Gospels is slightly superior to the rest, but as a whole, it is one of the best available.

THE NEW ENGLISH BIBLE. New Testament. New York: Cambridge University Press, 1961. Pp. 447. $4.95. Pap. $1.45.

This version aims to avoid the stilted diction and archaisms which have plagued previous translations. Therefore it is a free rendition but not a paraphrase, cast in the contemporary idiom. This text has been given official approbation of many Protestant churches.

NEW TESTAMENT. Revised Standard Version. Catholic edition. Collegeville, Minn.: Liturgical Press, 1965. $3.50.

This edition of the NT from the R.S.V. has been prepared for the use of Catholics by a committee of the Catholic Biblical Association of Great Britain. It is published with ecclesiastical approval. The NT of the R.S.V. was first published in 1946.

PHILLIPS, JOHN BERTRAM. *The Gospels translated into modern English.* New York: Macmillan, 1961. Pp. 252. Pap. $0.95.

A modern English translation, the aim of which was to recapture something of the style of the original texts by forgetting about previous translations.

_____. *The New Testament in modern English.* New York: Macmillan, 1958. $4.95. Pap. $1.95.

This is a translation made by a non-Catholic pastor in order to make the word of God intelligible to his parishioners.

2. Introduction to the New Testament

ALONSO SCHÖKEL, LUIS, S.J. *Journey through the Bible lands.* Translated by J. Drury. Milwaukee: Bruce, 1964. Pp. xii+346. $4.95.

Unlike some other travelogues of Palestine, this work presents a great deal of biblical geography and archeology to illustrate the texts concerned with the cities visited. The book is arranged according to the biblical chronology and has integrated much of recent research from scholarly books and periodicals.

HENSHAW, THOMAS. *New Testament literature in the light of modern scholarship.* New York: Humanities Press, 1952. Pp. 453. $6.00.

This work is not directed to scripture specialists but offers a good summary of the results of modern scholarship on the NT.

McNEILE, ALAN H. *An introduction to the study of the New Testament.* 2d ed., revised by C. S. C. Williams. New York: Oxford University Press, 1953. Pp. 486. $7.20.

Originally written for students at Oxford and now revised, this work is a standard tool in NT introduction. Noteworthy is the new section on form criticism.

MOULE, CHARLES FRANCIS D. *The birth of the New Testament.* New York: Harper and Row, 1962. Pp. xii+252. $5.00. (Harper's New Testament commentaries)

This book is not strictly a theology of the NT, although a number of theological issues come up for discussion. It tries to investigate the circumstances in the early Christian community which led to the composition of the NT.

TURNER, HENRY E. W. *Historicity and the Gospels:* a sketch of historical method and its application to the Gospels. Naperville, Ill.: Allenson, 1963. Pp. 108. $3.00.

This is the expansion of a lecture series given at Norwich Diocesan Clergy School. The author treats both historical and interpretative aspects of the Gospel.

WIKENHAUSER, ALFRED. *New Testament introduction.* Translated by J. Cunningham. New York: Herder and Herder, 1958. Pp. 580. $8.50. Pap. $4.95.

This introduction is of special interest to Protestants because the Catholic approach which it presents is quite different from what it was 50 years ago. It is the fruit of 30 years of the author's university teaching.

3. Harmonies

THE GOD-MAN JESUS: the life of Christ as recorded by the four evangelists. Compiled from the Kleist-Lilly version of the New Testament by Frank Dell'Isola. Milwaukee: Bruce, 1959. Pp. 238. $3.75.

The author has taken the Gospel passages and arranged them chronologically without comment or alteration to provide a Gospel harmony and a life of Christ.

A HARMONY OF THE GOSPELS IN KNOX TRANSLATION. Edited by L. Johnston and A. Pickering. New York: Sheed and Ward, 1963. Pp. 252. $6.00. Pap. $2.50.

As far as possible, the sequence of events in each Gospel were left in their own order. Indexes have been included to facilitate use.

HARTDEGEN, STEPHEN J., O.F.M. *A chronological harmony of the Gospels;* using the revised text of the Challoner-Rheims version of the New Testament. 3d ed. Paterson, N.J.: St. Anthony Guild Press, 1958. Pp. xxv+220. $2.50.

Except for the Bible text used, this is an excellent harmony with an outline of chronology, an index to each evangelist, an outline of our Lord's public ministry, notes on the genealogy and birth of Christ, a select bibliography, and other features to facilitate reading and understanding the Gospels.

IT IS PAUL WHO WRITES. Based on the translation of the Epistles of St. Paul and the Acts of the Apostles by Ronald Knox, arranged in a continuous narrative with explanations by Ronald Cox, C.M. New York: Sheed and Ward, 1959. Pp. 487. $4.50.

On the left hand pages is printed the continuous biblical text according to the Knox translation, and on the right hand pages is Cox's commentary. The Epistles are arranged in chronological sequence and interjected in seven points of the Acts. Father Cox's intention was to follow Paul's main line of thought and thus has refrained from giving various possible explanations of the text. The style is interesting and concrete; it will appeal to the general lay reader.

4. Commentaries and Exegesis of the Whole New Testament

MANSON, THOMAS WALTER. *Studies in the Gospels and Epistles.* Edited by M. Black. Philadelphia: Westminster Press, 1962. Pp. xvi+293. $6.50.

It should be noted that these studies are for those who have some understanding of NT exegesis and criticism. They will prove enlightening and stimulating. Some of the author's conclusions, however, are judged by scholars to be indefensible, particularly those of the seventh lecture dealing with the "Son of Man."

NEW TESTAMENT READING GUIDE. Edited by B. M. Ahern, C.P., K. Sullivan, R.S.C.J., and W. G. Heidt, O.S.B. 14 parts. Collegeville, Minn.: Liturgical Press, 1960. Pap. $0.30 each.

Popularly priced, this series presents the latest and soundest biblical scholarship in a brief, clear, and attractive way. The format is convenient because the upper part of each page contains the verses treated in the commentary at the bottom part of the same page. In length the booklets average about 100 pages each. Some of America's leading Catholic biblical scholars have collaborated in their production.

5. Commentaries on Individual Parts

a) Gospels

BEARE, FRANCIS WRIGHT. *The earliest records of Jesus;* a companion to The Synopsis of the First Three Gospels by Albert Huck. New York: Abingdon Press, 1962. Pp. 254. $6.50.

Some of the assumptions that the author makes, such as the priority of Mark, and Luke's independence from Matthew, may not be very well received by conservatives.

BOISMARD, MARIE EMILE, O.P. *St. John's Prologue.* Translated by the Carisbrooke Dominicans. Westminster, Md.: Newman Press, 1957. Pp. 152. $3.25.

An excellent study. The first part is a verse-by-verse commentary. The second part develops the central themes of the prologue and of Johannine theology. It unfolds before the reader some of the riches of a biblical theology not yet fully exploited.

BOUYER, LOUIS, C.Or. *The fourth Gospel.* Translated by Patrick Byrne. Westminster, Md.: Newman Press, 1964. Pp. 233. $4.50.

A convert from Lutheranism, Father Bouyer has dedicated this book to Oscar Cullmann to whom he feels indebted for his initiation into exegetical studies. In the treatment of the subject at hand he hardly ever delves deeply into technical matters, he doesn't argue, but he has a calm contemplative approach. He presents about 10 or 20 verses at a time, and then comments. It is thought-provoking and conducive to meditation.

BURKILL, T. ALEX. *Mysterious revelation;* an examination of the philosophy of St. Mark's Gospel. Ithaca, N.Y.: Cornell University Press, 1963. Pp. xii+337. $6.50.

Although there can be theological reservations about some of the author's conclusions, this book is a valuable contribution to the study of St. Mark's Gospel. Its main concern is the revelation of Christ's messiahship and the mysterious meaning of it.

CAIRD, GEORGE BRADFORD. *Gospel of St. Luke.* Baltimore: Penguin Books, 1964. Pp. 271. Pap. Pelican (A490) $1.65.

The Pelican Gospel series is meant to put the ordinary reader in touch with the findings of modern scholarship about the Gospels. The text is the R.S.V. There is first a general commentary paragraph by paragraph, and then points of detail are considered for each paragraph. The Catholic reader must be cautioned about this commentator's unacceptable theology in speaking of the virgin birth and the perpetual virginity of Mary.

CERFAUX, LUCIEN. *Apostle and apostolate, according to the Gospel of St. Matthew.* Translated by D. D. Duggan. New York: Desclee, 1960. Pp. 183. $2.75.

This is a commentary on the missionary discourse of our Lord in Matt. 10. The author reveals in clear and impassioned language the spiritual riches of the missiological admonitions of Christ and shows how they have been realized in saints like Francis of Assisi, Benedict Joseph Labre, and John Vianney.

_____. *The four Gospels:* an historical introduction. Translated by P. Hepburne-Scott. Westminster, Md.: Newman Press, 1960. Pp. 145. $3.00.

This work on the Gospels will serve as an excellent guide through the heated discussions on the Gospels in the last few years. It gives excellent summaries of non-Catholic criticism.

CRANFIELD, C. E. B. *The Gospel according to St. Mark.* New York: Cambridge University Press, 1950. Pp. xv+479. $7.50. Pap. $2.95. (Cambridge Greek Testament commentary)

This work, like others in the series, is characterized by its word study and doctrinal exposition. The author admits his dependence on former studies, particularly that of Vincent Taylor, but his conciseness serves to sharpen the focus. The approach is generally conservative.

DILLERSBERGER, JOSEF. *The Gospel of St. Luke.* Translated from the German. Westminster, Md.: Newman Press, 1958. Pp. xii+558. $5.75.

A penetrating analysis of the third Gospel's literary and devotional qualities. It provides deep spiritual insight for the ordinary reader, and even the scripture scholar will find the comments stimulating.

DODD, CHARLES HAROLD. *The interpretation of the Fourth Gospel.* New York: Cambridge University Press, 1953. Pp. xi+477. $9.50.

In the wake of the discoveries at Qumrân some scholars have concluded that the author of the Fourth Gospel was typically Jewish in his background and in his orientation. This author sees many Hellenistic influences. The work is scholarly and should be read with the Gospel text in hand.

FENTON, JOHN. *Gospel of St. Matthew.* Baltimore: Penguin Books, 1964. Pp. 487. Pap. Pelican (A488) $1.95.

As one might expect, this series on the Gospels inevitably comes face to face with the synoptic problem. Mr. Fenton is aware that the opinion that Matthew drew from Mark is not capable of a simple demonstration. Yet he does not hesitate to maintain that incidents found in Matthew and absent in Mark are to be attributed to Matthew's imagination "without historical evidence for them." Otherwise this work follows the same pattern as the others in the series and will prove equally useful.

FEUILLET, ANDRE, S.S. *Johannine studies.* New York: Herder and Herder, 1964. Pp. 292. $5.95.

Articles previously published by the author in learned journals are here collected in order to reach a greater number of readers. Perhaps the most outstanding of these articles is the one on St. John, chapter 6, and especially the relationship which the author sees in it to Wisdom literature. Not all scholars will agree with the author's conclusions, but certainly he has made a valuable contribution by these provocative studies.

HASTINGS, ADRIAN. *Prophet and witness in Jerusalem:* a study of the teaching of St. Luke. Baltimore: (Helicon) Taplinger, 1958. Pp. 198. $4.00.

Making use of the best in Catholic and Protestant biblical scholarship, the author has developed a thematic approach to the writings of St. Luke. His book focuses on Christ's prophetic character, his role as the new Elias, and the NT concept of witnessing.

LAGRANGE, MARIE JOSEPH, O.P. *The Gospel of Jesus Christ.* 2v. Translated from the French. New York: Newman Press, 1943. $6.00 each.

This is an English condensation of a larger work in 4 volumes. It is characterized by the author's attention to the literal meaning of the Gospel texts, and his vivid details of historical, archeological, and geographical background.

LIGHTFOOT, ROBERT HENRY. *The Gospel of St. Mark.* New York: Oxford University Press, 1952. Pp. 116. $5.00. Pap. $1.50.

Of special interest in this collection of lectures and articles is the chapter devoted to form criticism which shows its contribution to our understanding and interpretation of the Gospels. But the chief gain to the reader comes in a better understanding of some of the main themes of the Gospel.

MULLINS, ALOYSIUS, O.P. *A guide to the kingdom:* a simple handbook on the parables. Westminster, Md.: Newman Press, 1963. Pp. 139. $3.75.

As an aid to preachers, the former professor of Scripture at the Angelicum has divided the parables of the synoptics into dogmatic or doctrinal, and moral. He also treats allegories.

NINEHAM, DENNIS ERIC. *Gospel of St. Mark.* Baltimore: Penguin Books, 1964. Pp. 477. Pap. Pelican (A489) $1.95.

Like the other works of this series, there is a general commentary. Here, however, the author tends to be too radical in the principles which he enunciates. He flatly asserts the priority of Mark and draws conclusions from it as though it were a fact proven beyond dispute. He treats the question of historicity in the Gospels with some care, but will sometimes reject an incident as unhistorical without further comment. In spite of these shortcomings, a critical reader can derive much good from this work.

SHEED, FRANCIS J. *To know Christ Jesus.* New York: Sheed and Ward, 1962. Pp. xx+377. $5.00.

The object of this excellent exposition of the Gospels is not to prove something, but to introduce someone. The style is simple, the content profound.

TURNER, HENRY ERNEST WILLIAM. *Historicity and the Gospels;* a sketch of historical method and its application to the Gospels. Naperville, Ill.: Allenson, 1963. Pp. ix+108. $3.00.

Some Catholics will be scandalized at the fact that a scholar would even attempt to apply the historical method to the Gospels. However, Dr. Turner emphasizes the honesty of the evangelists, and he is not unaware that the account which we give of Christian origins has to bear some relation to the Christian story that derives from them. The book is a valuable contribution; at times even edifying.

VANN, GERALD, O.P. *The Eagle's Word;* a presentation of the Gospel according to St. John, with an introductory essay. New York: Harcourt, Brace and World, 1961. Pp. 247. $4.50.

The 211-page introduction explains John's imagery and symbolism. The discussion of John's key concepts, e.g., logos, life, light, is clear and succinct. The text itself is more of a paraphrase than a translation, and so helps the reader capture the richness and depth of the inspired author.

b) Epistles

BARCLAY, WILLIAM. *The all-sufficient Christ;* studies in Paul's Letter to the Colossians. Philadelphia: Westminster Press, 1963. Pp. 142. Pap. $1.45.

The author is a lecturer in New Testament and Greek at the University of Glasgow. His book is a layman's introduction to the Epistle to the Colossians.

BARRETT, CHARLES KINGSLEY. *A commentary on the Epistle to the Romans.* New York: Harper, 1958. Pp. 294. $4.00. (Harper's New Testament commentaries)

A very useful commentary; scholarship lucidly presented.

BEARE, FRANCIS WRIGHT. *A commentary on the Epistle to the Philippians.* New York: Harper, 1959. Pp. 182. $3.50. (Harper's New Testament commentaries)

A readable commentary which the non-specialist can apply to his personal life.

CODY, AELRED, O.S.B. *Heavenly sanctuary and liturgy in the Epistle to the Hebrews;* the achievement of salvation in the Epistle's perspectives. St. Meinrad, Ind.: Grail Publications, 1960. Pp. xiii+227. $5.00.

This doctoral thesis is suited to the exegete and theologian. We are currently being made aware, however, of the theological import of the resurrection. And here is a work that gives due emphasis to the ascension and heavenly enthronement of our Lord in heaven.

FOULKES, FRANCIS. *The Epistle of Paul to the Ephesians,* an introduction and commentary. Grand Rapids: Eerdmans, 1963. Pp. 181. $3.00. (Tyndale New Testament commentaries)

Clarity, conciseness, and readability are the chief characteristics of this work. The literary trappings of scholarship such as bibliographical apparatus are kept to a minimum in the interests of readability, but the author displays a familiarity of his subject and leaves no doubt about the soundness of his scholarship. The book contains nothing new but is a valuable guide for one who is approaching Ephesians for the first time.

*LAWLER, BRENDAN, S.J. *The epistles in focus.* Toronto: McClelland, 1954. Pp. 165. $3.25.

For many the epistles seem confusing and difficult to understand. This commentary clears the vision of the reader and leads him to the message of the sacred letters. The style is crisp and readable.

SCHELKLE, KARL HERMANN. *The Epistle to the Romans.* New York: Herder and Herder, 1964. Pp. 269. $4.95.

The author, a renowned theologian, has dispensed with critical apparatus in this book. His concern is a straightforward and clear explanation of Paul's thought.

c) Acts and Apocalypse

BARCLAY, WILLIAM. *Letters to the seven churches.* New York: Abingdon Press, 1958. Pp. 111. $2.00.

Two chapters are devoted to each of the seven churches of Apoc. 1:11. The author has aimed at making the letters as meaningful to modern readers as they were for their original recipients.

DUPONT, JACQUES, O.S.B. *The sources of the Acts.* Translated by K. Pond. New York: Herder and Herder, 1964. Pp. 180. $4.75.

The author makes a clear distinction between source criticism and form criticism. He has some new insights into how the Acts must have been conceived and committed to writing.

FERET, HENRI MARIE. *The Apocalypse of St. John.* Translated by E. Corathiel. Westminster, Md.: Newman Press, 1958. Pp. 273. $4.00.

The chief value of this book derives from the fact that its author is a historian as well as a theologian. He has some good insights into the philosophy of history and does much to obliterate many apprehensions held by lay readers concerning one of the great texts of Christian literature.

LILJE, HANS. *The last book of the Bible;* the meaning of the revelation of St. John. Translated by O. Wyon. Philadelphia: Fortress Press, 1957. Pp. 286. $4.75.

The author, the Evangelical Lutheran bishop of Hannover, wrote this book while a prisoner of the Gestapo. Part I gives general background; Part II is a commentary.

MARTINDALE, CYRIL C., S.J. *The Acts of the Apostles;* with an introduction and commentary. Westminster, Md.: Newman Press, 1958. Pp. 199. $3.00. (Stonyhurst Scripture manuals)

This is one of a series of scripture commentaries directed to students on the secondary level. Each manual contains a brief introduction and text (Douay version) with notes. The exegesis is sound with a minimum of controversial discussion.

*RICCIOTTI, GIUSEPPE. *The Acts of the Apostles.* Translated by L. E. Byrne. Milwaukee: Bruce, 1958. Pp. 420. $8.00, text edition, $6.00.

Those acquainted with some of the author's other writings will recognize in this book the high-level popularization. Defective orthography on the part of the printer mars the integrity of the author's good work.

SHEPHERD, MASSEY HAMILTON. *The paschal liturgy and the Apocalypse.* Richmond, Va.: John Knox Press, 1960. Pap. $1.75. (Ecumenical studies in worship, 6)

As the title implies, this work approaches the basic structure of the Book of Revelation. Through a survey of the development of the paschal rites and customs from the time of the Apostles to the beginning of the fourth century.

6. Biography

a) The Life of Christ

*AMIOT, FRANÇOIS, S.S. and others. *The sources for the life of Christ.* Translated by P. J. Hepburne-Scott. New York: Hawthorn Books, 1962. Pp. 128. $3.50. (Twentieth century encyclopedia of Catholicism, 67)

In seven essays, four biblical scholars discuss the sources for a biography of Christ.

BORNKAMM, GÜNTHER. *Jesus of Nazareth.* Translated by Irene and Frazer McClusky with J. M. Robinson. New York: Harper, 1960. Pp. 239. $4.00.

This is an appraisal of the synoptic Gospels. It is the work of a scholar, but reads very well, for the author makes references to classical writers, painters, musicians, or to the contemporary scene, and thus adds an interesting dimension. The book must be read critically, however, for we cannot accept the Jesus of history as completely different from the Christ of faith.

CARMICHAEL, JOEL. *The death of Jesus.* New York: Macmillan, 1963. Pp. 275. $4.95.

The author says that the nature of Christ's crime was sedition and insurrection. On this premise he attempts to explain the spread of Christianity.

GOODIER, ALBAN. *The public life of our Lord Jesus Christ.* 2v. New York: P. J. Kenedy, 1930. $12.50 set.

Inspired by his travels in the Holy Land, the author wrote a life of Christ which took the middle road between the devotional and the scientific. He attempts to answer the question, "What was our Lord like, as a man?"

GUARDINI, ROMANO. *The Lord.* Translated by E. C. Briefs. Chicago: H. Regnery Co., 1954. Pp. 535. $6.50.

With sound scholarship, Msgr. Guardini situates the life of Christ in the context of history. He also shows how the life of Christ relates to the Church today.

PRAT, FERNAND, S.J. *Jesus Christ, his life, his teachings, and his work.* Translated by J. J. Heenan, S.J. Milwaukee: Bruce, 1963. Pp. 542+568. $10.00.

When this work was originally published in two volumes M. J. Lagrange wrote: "It is outstanding . . . for a felicitous arrangement of its matter, a thorough familiarity with its subject, and a clear exposition of the teachings and the data of Jesus." This new one-volume arrangement eliminates the bulkiness of two volumes. Other new elements are the maps of Palestine on the end-pages and an extra index of references to the Sunday Gospels.

RICCIOTTI, GIUSEPPE. *The life of Christ.* Translated by A. I. Zizzania. Milwaukee: Bruce, 1947. Pp. 703. $8.25, text edition $5.70, popular edition $4.50.

The difference between the regular and abridged editions is that the latter omits the critical introduction. Both are readable, lucid, and scholarly in form.

SHEEN, FULTON J. *Life of Christ.* New York: McGraw-Hill, 1958. Pp. 559. $7.95.

This is not a simple re-telling of familiar incidents of Christ's life, but a dramatic and dynamic account of his significance as the God-man, a teacher of all ages and the Saviour of the world. It has been heralded as Bishop Sheen's greatest work, the fruit of more than 25 years of research.

SLOYAN, GERARD S. *Christ the Lord.* New York: Herder and Herder, 1962. Pp. 238. $4.50.

This life of Christ is not a theological reflection on the Gospel, but a quasi-paraphrase cast in colloquial style, all the while aiming at faithfulness to the literary form of the Gospel. The intended audience is the contemporary adolescent or students in secondary schools.

b) The Life of St. Paul

DANIEL-ROPS, HENRY. *Saint Paul: Apostle of nations.* Translated by J. Martin. Notre Dame, Ind.: Fides Publishers, 1963. Pp. 163. Pap. (D29) $0.95.

This scholarly biography of St. Paul is presented in a continuous narrative. It is an easy-to-read general introduction to the Pauline epistles.

HOLZNER, JOSEF. *Paul of Tarsus.* Translated by F. C. Eckhoff. St. Louis, Mo.: B. Herder Book Co., 1944. Pp. 502. $6.95.

Cast in a narrative style approximating the novel, this book makes available to a wide audience the fruits of Pauline scholarship without delving into the more thorny problems of textual exegesis.

RICCIOTTI, GIUSEPPE. *Paul the Apostle.* Milwaukee: Bruce, 1961. Pp. 540. $2.95.

Both the background and the historical narrative are derived from primary sources, but written in a style which approaches the informal.

7. New Testament Theology

AMIOT, FRANÇOIS, S.S. *The key concepts of St. Paul.* Translated by J. Dingle. New York: Herder and Herder, 1962. Pp. 297. $4.95.

Pauline doctrines are related to the theme of salvation through the crucified and risen Christ; the opening chapters are on the life and teaching of St. Paul.

BAUM, GREGORY, O.S.A. *The Jews and the Gospel;* a re-examination of the New Testament. Westminster, Md.: Newman Press, 1961. Pp. 288. $4.50.

The author writes on a timely subject. He maintains that any attempt to base anti-Semitism on the NT involves a distortion of the NT's genuine meaning.

CERFAUX, LUCIEN. *Christ in the theology of St. Paul.* Translated by G. Webb and A. Walker. New York: Herder and Herder, 1959. Pp. 560. $8.75.

The author shows the progression of Pauline thought in three successive syntheses: Christ the Saviour, the gift of Christ, the mystery of Christ.

_____. *The Church in the theology of St. Paul.* Translated by G. Webb and A. Walker. New York: Herder and Herder, 1959. Pp. 419. $6.50.

The author is not pre-occupied with a complete synthesis on the meaning of the word "Church," but with its origin and development in the mind of Paul from the scrutiny of pertinent ecclesiological formulas. Therefore some ecclesiologists have been critical. To wade through the three parts of this book and understand its contents requires a thorough familiarity with Greek expressions and an understanding of disputed questions of Pauline theology. This is no book for neophytes, but biblical theologians welcome it and profit much by reading it.

DURRWELL, FRANCIS XAVIER, C.SS.R. *The Resurrection;* a biblical study. Translated by R. Sheed. New York: Sheed and Ward, 1960. Pp. 371. $6.00.

This book went through five editions in French before it was translated into English. It confronts the reader with the fundamental mystery of Christianity and focuses sharply on the eschatological aspect of Christ's glory.

_____. *In the redeeming Christ;* towards a theology of spirituality. Translated by R. Sheed. New York: Sheed and Ward, 1963. Pp. 292. $5.00.

A worthy companion to the title immediately preceding, for the author applies the results of his exegetical study to themes of the spiritual life.

FAITH, REASON AND THE GOSPELS; a selection of modern thought on faith in the Gospels. Edited by J. J. Heaney, S.J. Westminster, Md.: Newman Press, 1961. Pp. 327. $4.95. Pap. $1.95.

This is an anthology of articles by Catholic and Protestant authors. It brings before the intelligent Christian some of the better thought in the area indicated by the title.

*GROSSOUW, WILLIAM KAREL MARIA. *In Christ;* a sketch of the theo
ogy of St. Paul. Translated by M. W. Schoenberg, O.S.C. Westminster
Md.: Newman Press, 1959. Pp. 138. $2.25.

This book was written for the average Catholic who wants a better under
standing of the leading ideas of St. Paul. The translator has edited the secon
Dutch edition and added notes of special interest to American readers.

——————————. *Revelation and redemption;* a sketch of the theology of St. John
Translated and edited by M. W. Schoenberg. Westminster, Md.: Newma
Press, 1955. Pp. 133. $2.25.

The author's purpose is to put the modern Catholic in touch with the
wealth of Johannine thought. In the first chapter he lays the foundation
by explaining John's distinctive genre, and in succeeding chapters he ex
plains the evangelist's leading ideas. He presupposes some familiarity with
the text.

JONES, GERAINT VAUGHAN. *Christology and myth in the New Testament*
an inquiry into the character, extent, and interpretation of the mytho
logical element in the New Testament chronology. London: Allen and
Unwin, 1956. Pp. 295. $4.25.

This is a fine exposé of Bultmann's process of demythologizing. The
author undertakes this work on the premise that the issues raised by Bult
mann are of major importance to modern theology, but he comes to his own
conclusions.

*MALEVEZ, LEOPOLD, S.J. *The Christian message and myth;* the theology
of Rudolf Bultmann. Translated by O. Wyon. Westminster, Md.: Newman
Press, 1960. Pp. 215. $4.50.

The author, a professor at St. Albert College, Louvain, ably explains and
criticizes Bultmann's principle of existential interpretation and especially
his program of demythologizing.

O'CONNOR, EDWARD DENNIS, C.S.C. *Faith in the synoptic Gospels;* a
problem in the correlation of scripture and theology. Notre Dame, Ind.
University of Notre Dame Press, 1961. Pp. 164. $4.00.

In this exegetical study of the Synoptics' concept of faith, the author tries
to put the findings of biblical theology into forms which will facilitate their
consideration by speculative theology.

PRAT, FERNAND, S.J. *The theology of Saint Paul.* 2v. Translated by
J. L. Stoddard. New York: Benziger Brothers, 1946. $10.00 set.

J. Daniélou recently sponsored the reprinting of this work in French
because it has not lost its relevance. Contemporary studies only tend to con
firm its conclusions. The author's philological background, solid erudition
and theological good sense render it a classic.

QUESNELL, QUENTIN, S. J. *This Good News;* an introduction to the Cath
olic theology of the New Testament. Milwaukee: Bruce, 1964. Pp. xiv+224.
$4.50. (Impact books)

Not only does this book sum up the Gospels, it also adapts them to
our times. It examines the minds of the evangelists and the commission of
Christ to preach to the whole world. It seeks to point out the new meaning
given to life, as a result of an encounter with Christ.

RICHARDSON, ALAN. *Introduction to the theology of the New Testament.*
New York: Harper, 1959. Pp. 423. $5.00.

The material of this book can be divided into three parts: theology,

Christology, and ecclesiology. Although the author has succeeded in conveying an immense amount of information in a form that is logical and lucid, he has been criticized by reputable scholars for his defective attitude toward miracles. He lacks any real sense of *heilsgeschichte,* that is, of salvific history as meaningful. Inspite of this weakness the book has been valuable to students of the New Testament because of its many strong points.

RYAN, SISTER ROSALIE, C.S.J. *Contemporary New Testament studies.* Collegeville, Minn.: Liturgical Press, 1965. Pp. 484. $5.50. Pap. $3.95.

This is a collection of essays whose purpose it is to bring together significant recent articles which reflect current trends in New Testament studies. It is intended for the adult non-specialist and therefore does not stress technical problems such as the synoptic problem, "demythologizing," and "sensus plenior." Here within the covers of one book we find a wealth of scholarship which will benefit the interested layman, study groups, and college students.

SCHNACKENBURG, RUDOLF. *God's rule and kingdom.* Translated by J. Murray. New York: Herder and Herder, 1963. Pp. 365. $6.95.

The book briefly traces the development of the concept of the kingdom of God through the OT into the intertestamental period. A second section treats of the NT. In this latter, the author's originality is revealed in his attempt to determine the historical teaching of Jesus on the kingdom.

————. *New Testament theology today.* Translated by D. Askew. New York: Herder and Herder, 1963. Pp. 133. $2.95.

The author, co-editor of *Biblische Zeitschrift,* presents a balanced evaluation of the central concerns of modern scholarship and a bibliographic guide. The fact that this book has been translated into several languages is evidence that it is highly valued by scholars.

SPICQ, CESLAUS, O.P. *Agape in the New Testament.* Translated by M. A. McNamara, and H. H. Richter, O.P. St. Louis, Mo.: B. Herder Book Co., 1963. Pp. 153. $3.50.

Another volume on the Johannine and other writings of the NT will complete this first volume, which treats only the agape texts of the synoptic Gospels. Father Spicq searches out each text in which the inspired authors used the terms love, to love, and beloved. He arranges them in chronological order and then analyzes each exhaustively in its context. Technical footnotes and bibliographical apparatus have been omitted in this translation.

————. *The Trinity and our moral life according to St. Paul.* Translated by Sister M. Aquinas, O.P. Westminster, Md.: Newman Press, 1963. Pp. 131. $2.75.

From the writings of Paul, the author shows the necessity for a revealed morality, coming from God the Father not as an abstract ethic, but in the person of Christ.

STANLEY, DAVID MICHAEL, S.J. *Christ's resurrection in Pauline soteriology.* Rome: Pontificio Instituto Biblico, 1961. Pp. 313. Pap. $6.50. (Analecta Biblica, 13)

In this revised scriptural dissertation, the author, who is professor of NT studies at Regis College, Ontario, has given us a key work for an understanding of the resurrection and its role in salvation history.

*TRESMONTANT, CLAUDE. *Saint Paul and the mystery of Christ.* Translated by D. Attwater. New York: Harper, 1957. Pp. 190. $1.65.

The approach is more historical and philosophical than exegetical. The work can serve as a sort of survey course in biblical theology; it is a stimulating introduction.

WIKENHAUSER, ALFRED. *Pauline mysticism;* Christ in the mystical teaching of St. Paul. Translated by J. Cunningham. New York: Herder and Herder, 1960. Pp. 256. $4.50.

The author's analysis of Pauline mysticism is based on key texts, taken collectively and singly, which express the union of Christ and his members.

WINKLHOFER, ALOIS. *The coming of his kingdom;* a theology of the last things. Translated by A. V. Littledale. New York: Herder and Herder, 1963. Pp. 254. $4.95.

This book is not written in a heavy theological style and it presents a reasonably thorough account of what God has revealed concerning the consummation of our individual lives and of the world.

E. PERTINENT PAPAL DOCUMENTS

ROME AND THE STUDY OF SCRIPTURE. 6th ed. St. Meinrad, Ind.: Grail Press, 1960. Pp. 138. Pap. $1.00.

A collection of the three great encyclicals of 1893, 1920, and 1943 on the study of sacred scripture, plus decisions by the Biblical Commission.

II
SYSTEMATIC THEOLOGY

A. INTRODUCTIONS AND GENERAL WORKS

CONGAR, YVES MARIE-JOSEPH, O.P. *Lay people in the Church.* Translated by D. Attwater. Westminster, Md.: Newman Press, 1957. Pp. 447. $6.75.

Father Congar's book is a real contribution towards a theology of the laity, i.e., a solid, scientific clarification of the position of the laity in the Church.

DAVIS, CHARLES. *Theology for today.* New York: Sheed and Ward, 1963. Pp. 310. $5.00.

These essays touch on major topics, ranging from apologetics to eschatology. They help pull together the threads of contemporary developments and enable the reader to acquire a balanced viewpoint.

DE WOLF, LOTAN HAROLD. *The case for theology in liberal perspective.* Philadelphia: Westminster Press, 1959. Pp. 206. $3.50.

Liberal perspective is proper to both Protestant and Catholic theology. Here a Protestant is writing and many of the points that he makes on subjects like the Word of God, God's concern for us, or the people of God, could be very well received by Catholics.

DIEM, HERMANN. *Dogmatics.* Translated by H. Knight. Philadelphia: Westminster Press, 1959. Pp. 375. $6.95.

Dogmatics is cast in quite a different mold with Protestants than with Catholics. Thus, much of this book is concerned with scriptural criticism. It is enlightening, but in order to understand and evaluate it one must possess a good grasp of Catholic theology.

DOORNIK, N. G. M. Van. *The meeting with Christ.* Translated and adapted by J. Paton. New York: P.J. Kenedy, 1964. Pp. xii+237. $4.95.

This book can help non-Catholics answer many questions concerning Catholicism. Catholics, on the other hand, will be aided to a more mature and penetrating knowledge of their faith. All readers will find that it is a wide-ranging work, well organized, and written in adult terms.

GERKEN, JOHN D., S.J. *Toward a theology of the layman.* New York: Herder and Herder, 1963. Pp. 152. $3.95.

This is a well-documented survey giving particular attention to the writings of Karl Rahner and Yves Congar. It serves as a stimulating theological discussion on matters considered by Vatican II.

KÜNG, HANS. *The Council in action;* theological reflections on the Second Vatican Council. Translated by C. Hastings. New York: Sheed and Ward, 1963. Pp. 276. $4.50.

This work, growing out of Father Küng's role as a *peritus* at the Council, consists of lectures and briefings given at Rome to numerous meetings of bishops, at pontifical colleges, to press conferences, etc.

NEWMAN, JOHN HENRY CARDINAL. *On consulting the laity in matters of doctrine.* Edited by J. Coulson. New York: Sheed and Ward, 1962. Pp. iv+118. $3.00.

Not reprinted in its entirety since 1859, this essay proposes the necessary role of the laity in the Church. It is written in the style of its time, but its message is contemporary and relevant.

PHILIPS, GERARD. *The role of the laity in the Church.* Translated by J.A. Gilbert and J. Moudry. Chicago: Fides Publishers, 1955. Pp. 175. $3.25.

Some roles of the laity which are treated are: Catholic Action, the laity's power of Orders, the laity and the Magisterium. A valuable synthesis of material otherwise not easily available.

QUIGLEY, MARTIN, Jr. and CONNORS, EDWARD M. *Catholic Action in practice:* family life, education, international life. New York: Random House, 1963. Pp. x+240. $4.95.

Some exceptions can be taken on minor points of accuracy, but as an introduction to the lay apostolate, this book is highly recommended. Both authors are eminently qualified to write on their subjects because of their years of experience.

RAHNER, KARL, S.J. *Theology for renewal.* New York: Sheed and Ward, 1965. Pp. 183. $4.00.

Father Rahner clearly explains the theology underlying some of the concepts discussed at Vatican II such as collegiality, restoration of deacons, the nature of the secular priesthood, and the role of the layman in the Church. The book is written for the non-specialist and is ecumenical in spirit.

SALET, GASTON, S.J. *The wonders of our faith.* Translated by J. Leonard. Westminster, Md.: Newman Press, 1961. Pp. 187. $3.50.

An extraordinary book in that it was written for those whose religious knowledge has not kept abreast of their professional knowledge. The author has taken the great Christian dogmas and shown them to be a source of light and life for ordinary Christians; he has expressed his ideas in language remarkably free of scholastic terminology.

SCHMAUS, MICHAEL. *The essence of Christianity.* Translated by J. H. Smith. Chicago: Scepter, 1961. Pp. xiv+288. $3.95.

This modern treatise by the much revered Munich theologian combines a mastery of theology with an appreciation of the vital issues of our times. Hence its aim and character is similar to Karl Adam's *Spirit of Catholicism.* In a popular form the author unfolds the theology of his major work, *Dogmatik,* with lucidity and order.

SHEED, FRANCIS JOSEPH. *Theology for beginners.* New York: Sheed and Ward, 1957. Pp. 241. $3.00.

The title of this book could be misleading, for although it will delight beginners, it will also please and reward the more advanced student of theology, for it presents in a new and refreshing style what he has long known and loved. The author is at his best in speaking of the Trinity. Much of what he says on the subject here can be found in one of his earlier works, *Theology and Sanity.*

WEIGEL, GUSTAVE and MADDEN, ARTHUR G. *Religion and the knowledge of God.* Englewood Cliffs, N.J.: Prentice-Hall, 1961. Pp. 118. $3.95. Pap. $1.95.

Subjects such as phenomenology and religion, or philosophical problems of mysticism and religious experience, which are treated by these authors are usually discussed only in book-lined studies. The fact that they have received but the scantest attention from American philosophers justifies their presentation in this book.

B. TRINITY

AUGUSTINUS, AURELIUS, SAINT. *The Trinity.* Translated by S. Mc-Kenna, C.SS.R. Washington, D.C.: Catholic University Press, 1963. Pp. xvii+539. $7.95. (The Fathers of the Church, 45)

The only other English translation available is that of Arthur West Hadden, published in 1873. This alone justifies its inclusion here, for it makes available one of Augustine's finest theological essays.

DEWAR, LINDSAY. *The Holy Spirit and modern thought;* an inquiry into the historical, theological and psychological aspects of the Christian doctrine of the Holy Spirit. New York: Harper, 1960. Pp. xvi+224. $4.50.

The reinterpretation of the doctrine of the Holy Spirit provides a starting point for this Anglican canon's study. His approach is through scripture, the Fathers, and modern psychology.

HENRY, ANTONIN M., O.P., ed. *God and his creation.* Chicago: Fides Publishers, 1954. Pp. xi+511. $5.50. (Theology Library, 2)

The outline of the series follows the general plan of the *Summa,* with this volume treating of the nature of God. It is well adapted to our time. The reflections and perspectives provided at the end of each chapter are welcomed by the clergy and educated laity who want to gain a deeper understanding of their faith.

JANSSENS, ALOYSIUS. *The mystery of the Trinity.* Fresno, Calif.: Academy Library Guild, 1954. Pp. 168. Pap. $1.95.

Herein one can find a handy, complete and yet not too diffuse exposition of the traditional mind of the Church on the Trinity. The approach is scriptural.

McDONOUGH, WILLIAM K. *The divine family;* the Trinity and our life in God. New York: Macmillan, 1963. Pp. x+178. $3.95.

This is a synthesis of the spiritual life based on our life of grace in the Trinity. The author presents the inner life of the triune God and our divine adoption.

*MARMION, COLUMBA, O.S.B. *The Trinity in our spiritual life;* an anthology of the writings of Dom Columba Marmion. Westminster, Md.: Newman Press, 1953. Pp. xxii+284. $3.50.

These texts presenting Dom Marmion's doctrine on the Trinity have been culled from other published works of the Abbot. He very aptly points up the implications of this doctrine in relationship to the soul of the Christian.

PIAULT, BERNARD. *What is the Trinity?* Translated by R. Haughton. New York: Hawthorn Books, 1959. Pp. 156. $3.50. (Twentieth century encyclopedia of Catholicism, 17)

The brevity of treatment does not in this case imply superficiality. In three parts the author treats: the OT preparation; the revelation of the NT; and the development during succeeding centuries in the East and West, which sought a deeper penetration and clearer formulation of the mystery.

*PRESTIGE, GEORGE LEONARD. *God in patristic thought.* London: S.P.C.K. Press, 1952. Pp. xxxiv+318. $4.00.

This is a by-product of an extensive research project for a Greek lexicon on all words relating to the doctrines of the Trinity and Incarnation. Its use presupposes some familiarity with these topics. The author helps dispel certain pre-conceptions about the Greek Fathers and gives them credit for supporting monotheism.

SPICQ, CESLAUS, O.P. *The Trinity and our moral life according to St. Paul.* [See Page 29.]

SULLIVAN, JOHN EDWARD. *The image of God:* the doctrine of St. Augustine and its influence. Dubuque, Ia.: Priory Press, 1963. Pp. 356. $5.00.

This is perhaps the first systematic investigation into St. Augustine's teaching about the image of the Trinity in man. The author has probed the originality of Augustine and made an attempt to estimate his influence on his successors, chiefly Aquinas.

C. CHRISTOLOGY

ADAM, KARL. *The Christ of faith.* Translated by Joyce Crick. New York: Pantheon, 1957. Pp. x+364. $6.00. Pap. Mentor (MQ430) $0.95.

This work is a summary of lectures which the author gave over a number of years at the University of Tübingen. He was not so concerned with the extension of academic theology as with bringing into relief the personal values which can be derived from the development of the Church's theology. The translation is defective in parts.

—————. *Christ our brother.* Translated by J. McCann, O.S.B. New York: Macmillan, 1938. Pp. vi+210. $3.50. Pap. Collier, $0.95.

The author takes one central Christian doctrine, the humanity of Christ, and attempts to present its practical implications. This book has become a classic in Christology.

—————. *The Son of God.* Translated by Philip Hereford. New York: Doubleday, 1960. Pp. 235. Pap. $0.95.

Although first published more than 30 years ago, this book has lost little of its prestige. Hardly anything written since has surpassed it or even appreciably elaborated on its basic ideas. Unfortunately the translation is sometimes inaccurate.

BORNKAMM, GÜNTHER. *Jesus of Nazareth.* Translated by Irene and F. McLuskey. [See page 25.]

*CERFAUX, LUCIEN. *Christ in the theology of St. Paul.* [See page 27.]

CULLMANN, OSCAR. *The Christology of the New Testament.* Rev. ed. Philadelphia: Westminster Press, 1964. Pp. 346. $6.50.

The author systematically investigates the most important titles given to Christ by NT writers relative to 1) his earthly life, 2) his eschatological function, 3) his glorified existence contemporaneous with the Church, and 4) his pre-existent state.

DANIÉLOU, JEAN, S.J. *Christ and us.* Translated by W. Roberts. New York: Sheed and Ward, 1961. Pp. 236. $3.95.

By speaking of the Jesus of history, or the Christ of faith, scholars have tended to compartmentalize Christ. Here Father Daniélou insists that we must approach Christ by evaluating his position in the whole economy of salvation history. Once this position is established, our approach to Christ will be essentially integrated.

DAWE, DONALD G. *The form of a servant:* a historical analysis of the kenotic motif. Philadelphia: Westminster Press, 1963. Pp. 218. $4.50.

This book explores the tradition that the Incarnation was an act of divine self-emptying or limitation, and applies consequences of this tradition to the construction of a contemporary Christology.

DIBELIUS, MARTIN. *Jesus.* Translated by C. B. Henrick and F. C. Grant. Philadelphia: Westminster Press, 1949. Pp. 160. $2.50.

Known equally as an eminent exegete for his studies on form criticism, and as a devout Christian believer, the Protestant author approaches the study of Jesus in a way that is markedly different from the demythologizing of Bultmann or the rationalism of Reisenstein.

DURRWELL, FRANCIS XAVIER, C.SS.R. *In the redeeming Christ;* toward a theology of spirituality. [See Page 27.]

*FELDER, HILARION, O.F.M. Cap. *Jesus of Nazareth.* Translated by B. Bittle, O.F.M. Cap. Milwaukee: Bruce, 1954. Pp. xii+353. $4.75.

Written from the point of view of apologetics, this book could arm the reader against the rationalist approach to the historical Jesus. It would not sustain the interest of the reader if read straight through, but it could be a good source for finding information concerning Christology.

GARRIGOU-LAGRANGE, REGINALD, O.P. *Christ the Savior.* St. Louis: B. Herder Book Co., 1956. Pp. 948. $6.00.

This work enables the priest engaged in parochial work or teaching to explain the primary and secondary questions of faith related to the Incarnation. Though it is not very readable, it is comprehensive.

GRAHAM, AELRED, O.S.B. *The Christ of Catholicism.* Garden City, N. Y.: Doubleday, 1957. Pp. 350. Pap. Image (D48) $0.95.

This book might well be characterized as a spiritual-dogmatic guide to the subject of Christology. It is a synthesis of the scriptural testimony and the dogmatic teaching of the Church on the most vital of all questions: "What think you of Christ? Whose Son is He?"

GUARDINI, ROMANO. *Jesus Christus;* meditations. Translated by P. White. Chicago: H. Regnery Co., 1959. Pp. 111. $2.75.

While these are truly meditations, they contain the wealth of theology which one would expect from this renowned theologian.

*HERIS, VINCENT, O.P. *The mystery of Christ, our head, priest and king.* Translated by D. Fahey. Westminster, Md.: Newman Press, 1950. Pp. 214. $3.50.

These pages are devoted chiefly to the study of the sovereign priesthood of Jesus. They attempt to explain how Christ exercised his priesthood and how he instituted the worship which he perpetuated through the extension of his priesthood in time. The approach is Thomistic; it may not readily engage the general reader, but can serve as a valuable survey for the initiated.

SCHLITZER, ALBERT, C.S.C. *Redemptive Incarnation;* sources and their theological development in the study of Christ. 3d ed. Notre Dame, Ind.: University of Notre Dame Press, 1962. Pp. xvi+438. $4.00.

Previous editions of this work have been up-dated with advances in biblical theology. The up-dating is especially notable in the treatment of the

OT preparation for the redemptive work of Christ, in chapter one. While this work does not embody much original scholarship, it is certainly a valuable contribution as a readable compendium.

D. GRACE

CUTTAZ, CANON F. *Our life of grace.* Translated by A. Bouchard. Chicago: Fides Publishing Co., 1958. Pp. vii+327. $5.95.

The primary objective of the author is to inspire the reader to a greater love for sanctifying grace. While his book is indeed inspirational, it is also doctrinal and readable, a clear and rather complete exposition of the effects of sanctifying grace.

DAUJAT, JEAN. *The theology of grace.* Translated by Sister Anselma Brennel. New York: Hawthorn Books, 1959. Pp. 158. $2.95.

The dictum that the supernatural builds on the natural was obviously observed in the arrangement of this book, for a good portion of it is devoted to the consideration of the endowments and limitations of human nature. Only then does the author proceed to give a rather complete overview of all that is revealed concerning grace.

FARRELLY, M. JOHN, O.S.B. *Predestination, grace and free will.* Westminster, Md.: Newman Press, 1964. Pp. xiv+317. $6.95.

The purpose of this study is to examine the harmony that exists between the primacy of God and the freedom of man, as regards man's movement toward his eternal fulfillment. A fresh study of this long controverted mystery is justified by the recent advances in biblical and doctrinal theology.

FRANSEN, PIET F., S.J. *Divine grace and man.* New York: Desclee, 1962. Pp. 117. $2.25.

None of the facts of modern psychology are lost in the author's treatment of grace. He distinguishes layers of depth within the person and his response to the encounter with the divine life. This makes exciting and dynamic reading for anyone concerned with a deeper knowledge of grace.

GLEASON, ROBERT W., S.J. *Grace.* New York: Sheed and Ward, 1962. Pp. viii+240. $3.95. Pap. $2.95.

This book expresses the most sublime concepts in terms easily comprehensible to the layman. It will be a useful guide to the seminarian, and it will be of service to the pastor who wants to present his people with the meaning of a personal encounter with Christ.

GUARDINI, ROMANO. *Freedom, grace and destiny;* three chapters in the interpretation of existence. Translated by J. Murray. New York: Pantheon Books, 1961. Pp. 384. $4.00.

Guardini shows us how God's revelation in Christ has transformed impersonal, irresponsible destiny into the responsible providence of our Father. The Christian accepts his life and his death as a gift in Christ.

JOURNET, CHARLES. *The meaning of grace.* Translated by A. V. Littledale. New York: P. J. Kenedy, 1960. Pp. 127. $3.50.

The author's intention in these discourses is to discuss answers to certain questions posed by the mystery of grace and to do so simply. He was successful in his efforts, particularly for non-theologians.

*JOYCE, GEORGE HAYWARD, S.J. *The Catholic doctrine of grace.* Westminster, Md.: Newman Press, 1950. Pp. xiv+267. $2.50.

The present book was written to meet the needs of readers who are theologically untrained. It sets forth the Church's teaching on grace in terms that are non-technical and it avoids becoming bogged down with historical controversies.

*MATTHEWS, JOHN V., S.J. *The life that is grace.* Westminster, Md.: Newman Press, 1953. Pp. vii+196. $2.50.

A work of piety written by a theologian. It is the author's concern to make theology meaningful for Christians who do not formally study Christian doctrine. He has taken the essence of theology and expressed it simply, as well as vitally.

NICOLAS, JEAN H., O.P. *The mystery of God's grace.* Translated from the French. Dubuque, Iowa: Priory Press, 1960. Pp. x+102. Pap. $1.25.

Although this little book did not receive very extensive reviews, it is definitely a contribution to the theology of grace, if not in its originality at least in its organization. In three parts it sets out to answer the questions: What is grace? Where does grace come from? Where does grace lead?

*SHEEBEN, MATTHIAS JOSEPH, S.J. *Nature and grace.* Translated by C. Vollert, S.J. St. Louis, Mo.: B. Herder Book Co., 1954. Pp. xxiv+361. $4.95.

This book has been held in high esteem, but more for its depth and erudition than for its clarity and precision. Even at that it is one of the best and most stimulating studies on nature and grace, and has lost little of its significance in the years since it was first published in the German original.

STEVENS, PETER GREGORY, O.S.B. *The life of grace.* Englewood Cliffs, N.J.: Prentice-Hall, 1963. Pp. viii+118. $3.95. Pap. $1.50.

The significance of this book is that it harmonizes systematic theology with the data of sacred scripture. The author begins with citations from the NT and shows how greater theological precision was instigated by later heresies.

E. THE SACRAMENTS

1. Sacraments in general

BOUYER, LOUIS, C.Or. *Word, Church and sacraments in Protestantism and Catholicism.* Translated by A. V. Littledale. New York: Desclee, 1961. Pp. 80. $2.00.

Father Bouyer here continues his apostolate of reconciliation between Catholic and Protestant. This book is directed mainly at the enlightenment of the Catholic. The sacraments are considered not only as means of grace, but as the activity of Christ through his Holy Spirit.

FRANSEN, PIET F., S.J. *Faith and the sacraments.* New York: Hillary, 1958. Pp. 30. $1.00. (Aquinas papers, 31)

A scholarly essay divided into three parts: 1) a short outline of theological thought which governs modern research in this area; 2) discussion of St. Thomas, as put forth by Father Schillebeeckx; 3) presentation of the principal elements of symbolic activity as a characteristic of human activity in general.

HASTINGS, CECILY. *The sacraments.* New York: Sheed and Ward, 1961. Pp. 217. $3.50.

In a style which is crisp, fresh and without a wasted word, the author presents a work of high-level popularization. She could not have been so successful without a broad familiarity with scholarly work. The first third of the book treats of general sacramental doctrine, and the remaining two-thirds is devoted to individual sacraments.

HENRY, ANTONIN M., O.P., ed. *Christ in his sacraments.* Translated by A. Bouchard. Chicago: Fides Publishers, 1958. Pp. 465. $5.00. (Theology library, 6)

The chapters of this book were written by various authors. The coherence of the work does not seem to have suffered, while the depth and excellence of it were greatly enhanced. The emphasis on the sacraments is more on liturgy and on faith in the recipient than on causality.

HOWELL, CLIFFORD, S.J. *Of sacraments and sacrifice.* Collegeville, Minn.: Liturgical Press, 1952. Pp. xi+171. $2.00. Pap. $0.90.

Professional theologians may raise eyebrows as Father Howell explains the Mass in terms of chemical experiments or a lemon pie, but he is not writing for professional theologians. While the terminology is comprehensible, the theology is also solid. Those who have difficulty in accepting the recent liturgical reforms may benefit from a reading of Part II, chapters 5 and 6.

LEEMING, BERNARD. *Principles of sacramental theology.* Rev. ed. Westminster, Md.: Newman Press, 1956. Pp. lvii+690. $6.95.

Father Leeming's treatise on sacraments is general and thorough. Throughout he gives evidence of his wide and sympathetic reading of Protestant literature and points out that the sacraments can be a point of meeting for divided Christians. He treats of the efficacy of the sacraments, sacramental character, sacramental causality, institution of the sacraments, requirements in the minster, and sacramental economy. This is not milk for babes, but meat for men. The layman without theological training could stagger through the preface, but he would not finish chapter one.

MARTIMORT, AIMÉ GEORGES. *The signs of the new covenant.* Collegeville, Minn.: Liturgical Press, 1963. Pp. xiv +320. $4.75.

This work was first drafted at the request of the Christian Brothers to provide a theology course on the sacraments for junior religious. Thus it answers the need for solid doctrinal formation while avoiding any excessively technical presentation.

O'CALLAGHAN, DENIS, ed. *Sacraments, the gestures of Christ.* New York: Sheed and Ward, 1965. Pp. 194. $4.00.

In this book the theological considerations of the sacraments are updated and refurbished. While its content is an enlightening challenge to the clergyman, its terminology is also comprehensible to the layman.

O'NEILL, COLMAN E., O.P. *Meeting Christ in the sacraments.* Staten Island, N.Y.: Alba House, 1964. Pp. 371. $4.95.

The author takes his theme for this book from the *Constitution on the Sacred Liturgy:* "Christ is always present in his church, especially in her liturgical actions." Just how Christ is present is a delicate question which he takes every care to discuss with clarity and precision. Not every problem is solved but sacramental theology and a vital sacramental piety have been advanced through the publication of this book.

PALMER, PAUL F., ed. *Sacraments of worship.* Westminster, Md.: Newman Press, 1955. $4.75. (Sources of Christian theology, 1)

The liturgical and doctrinal development of baptism, confirmation and the Eucharist presented through translations of basic texts which have shaped and continue to influence Catholic theology. The selections range from Justin to the present. Five main topics are included in this volume: 1) early rites and initiation, 2) early Eucharistic liturgies, 3) the sacramental system, 4) Eucharist as sacrament, 5) Eucharist as sacrifice.

_____. *Sacraments of healing and vocation.* Englewood Cliffs, N.J.: Prentice-Hall, 1963. Pp. ix+118. $3.95. (Foundations of Catholic Theology)

This volume is part of the series, Foundations of Catholic Theology, which is aimed at students on the college level. The methodology of presentation of this title is similar to that followed by the author in his larger work cited above. Part I contains a chapter on penance and a chapter on extreme unction; Part II contains a chapter on the sacrament of order and a chapter on the sacrament of matrimony. These sacraments are viewed in their scriptural setting, in the teachings of the Fathers and in the teachings of the Post-Tridentine Church.

ROGUET, AIMO M., O.P. *Christ acts through sacraments.* Collegeville, Minn.: Liturgical Press, 1954. Pp. 162. Pap. $1.25.

From this book one can gain a more profound appreciation for sacramental signs and for the activity of Christ present in each sacrament. The contents are soundly theological but popularly phrased, since their original form was that of lectures and radio addresses.

SCHILLEBEECKX, EDWARD, O.P. *Christ the sacrament of the encounter with God.* New York: Sheed and Ward, 1963. Pp. 222. $4.50.

From the Bible and the Fathers, the author constructs his theology of the sacraments. He discusses the actions of the life of Christ, the primordial sacrament; he interprets the Church as the extension of Christ in time, and shows that the sacraments administered by the Church are a sharing in the mysteries of Christ's life.

TARDIF, HENRI. *The sacraments are ours.* Translated by A. Dean. London: Challoner, 1956. Pp. v+89. $1.00.

A studious work which presents Christian doctrine primarily from the standpoint of the liturgist. Leading ideas in the book: each sacrament is an act of worship; the corporate nature of life in the Church; the individual work of each man's sanctification through the sacraments.

*TAYMANS D'EYPERNON. *The Blessed Trinity and the sacraments.* Westminster, Md.: Newman Press, 1961. Pp. 150. $3.50.

Father d'Eypernon is a professor of theology at the University of Louvain. He devotes the first two chapters to the effects and causality of the sacraments and the manner in which Christ is present in them. The Eucharist is treated in the last chapter; it is here especially that the Trinitarian aspect of the sacraments is dealt with.

2. Individual Sacraments

a) Baptism

BOUYER, LOUIS, C. Or. *Christian initiation.* New York: Macmillan, 1960. Pp. 148. $3.25.

Some have observed that the chief value of this book lies in the original "asides" which are developed in working out the discovery of Christian life.

CREHAN, JOSEPH. *Early Christian baptism and the creed.* London: Burns and Oates, 1950. Pp. x+189. $2.95.

An attempt has been made in this work to limit the evidence for the origins of the Creed to ancient sources. An examination of the early history of baptism and its relation to the Creed does not lead the reader to any shocking conclusions, but it will give him a deeper appreciation of baptism.

CUTTAZ, FRANÇOIS. *Baptism: divine birth.* Staten Island, N.Y.: Alba House, 1962. Pp. viii+239. $3.95.

This book may be described as a theological, liturgical and ascetical commentary on the effects of baptism. Part I, the more important, deals with the effects of baptism; Part II, with the consequences which derive from the effects.

DAVIS, CHARLES. *Sacraments of initiation: baptism and confirmation.* New York: Sheed and Ward, 1964. Pp. 159. $3.50.

Unlike a dogma textbook, the author does not merely cite opinions but states which opinion he makes his own. He traces the origin of the sacraments of baptism and confirmation and ends with a summary of present practice. Through it all he interjects ascetical comments which will enable the priest to make the ceremonies more meaningful for the people attending.

DELORME, JEAN and others. *Baptism in the New Testament.* Baltimore, Md.: (Helicon) Taplinger, 1964. Pp. 238. $4.50.

This book consists of nine essays by outstanding theologians and scholars who reveal the profound meaning of the sacrament of initiation. It promotes and reflects the new prominence given to the sacraments as a result of the liturgical renewal.

*FLEMINGTON, W. F. *The New Testament doctrine of baptism.* London: S.P.C.K. Press, 1953. Pp. x+160. $1.75.

The first part of the book deals with the antecedents of Christian baptism. The author sees ethnic parallels in practically every human culture and period, but concludes, "Analogy does not mean genealogy." The remaining two parts supply a rather extensive study of baptismal texts in the NT.

NEUNHEUSER, BURKHARD. *Baptism and confirmation.* New York: Herder and Herder, 1964. Pp. 251. $6.50.

A study of baptism and confirmation that gives evidence of much research. The author traces each sacrament through the patristic period, the scholastic era of formulation, the counter-reformation and the modern renaissance of sacramental theology.

PLUS, RAOUL, S.J. *Baptism and confirmation.* Westminster, Md.: Newman Press, 1961. Pp. 101. Pap. $1.50.

A practical and helpful work. It sets out in simple terms the teaching of the Church on these two sacraments. The far greater portion of the book is devoted to baptism, for only the last chapter treats of confirmation.

SCHNACKENBURG, RUDOLF. *Baptism in the thought of St. Paul.* New York: Herder and Herder, 1964. Pp. 240. $5.95.

An exposition of the theology of baptism through a scrutiny of Pauline texts referring to the sacrament and of themes such as the new man, incorporation in Christ, and salvation event.

b) Confirmation

BOHEN, MARIAN, O.S.U. *The mystery of confirmation.* New York: Herder and Herder, 1963. Pp. 192. $4.50.

This book grew from its author's concern over the apathy of confirmed Christians, who should be zealous to renew the face of the earth. Her deeper study of the sacrament reveals dimensions rarely found in treatises on confirmation.

*THORNTON, LIONEL. *Confirmation:* its place in the baptismal mystery. Westminster, Md.: Dacre, 1954. Pp. xiv+204. $2.25.

Here an Anglican investigates the historical background for the sacrament of confirmation through early Christian documents such as the Apostolic Tradition of Hippolytus, and those of the earlier Jewish rites. The author has done much to aid scholars in establishing liturgical and theological contexts of the sacrament.

THURIAN, MAX. *Consecration of a layman;* new approaches to the sacrament of confirmation. Translated by W. J. Kerrigan. Baltimore, Md.: (Helicon) Taplinger, 1963. Pp. 118. $2.95.

The author is a member of the Protestant monastic community of Taizé, but shows no sign of the traditional Protestant polemic against sacramental theology. Here his approach to the sacraments of baptism and confirmation is ecumenical in character, but he by no means presents a Catholic theology of confirmation. While many authors may disagree with him, the general effect of the questions which he raises and attempts to answer, will be another step toward Church unity.

c) Penance

ANCIAUX, PAUL *The sacrament of penance.* New York: Sheed and Ward, 1962. Pp. 190. $3.50.

The scope of this book is the historical, doctrinal, and pastoral questions involved in the sacrament of penance. Except for the Latin quotations and citations in Dutch, it is well suited to the lay reader.

BARTON, JOHN. *Penance and absolution.* New York: Hawthorn Books, 1961. Pp. 157. $3.50. (Twentieth century encyclopedia of Catholicism, 51)

While the author has succeeded in presenting his reader with a compendium on the sacrament of penance which gives evidence of a familiarity with modern studies on the subject, it is regrettable that an emphasis on the canonical and moral aspects works to the detriment of the liturgical and social aspects of the sacrament.

PALMER, PAUL F., ed. *Sacraments and forgiveness.* Westminster, Md.: Newman Press, 1960. Pp. 410. $6.00. (Sources of Christian theology, 2)

This is a topical arrangement of basic texts on penance, extreme unction and indulgences. It is a real vademecum of primary source materials.

POSCHMANN, BERNHARD. *Penance and the anointing of the sick.* Translated and revised by F. Courtney, S.J. New York: Herder and Herder, 1964. Pp. 257. $6.50.

This book is chiefly a history of the administration of the sacrament of penance with some space devoted to indulgences and the anointing of the sick. The author lays special stress on the sacrament of penance as a reconciliation with the Church. This is a theological evaluation of an interpretation and it will be a valuable addition to the priest's personal library.

RIGA, PETER. *Sin and penance;* insights into the mystery of salvation. Milwaukee: Bruce, 1962. Pp. xv+187. $4.25.

Historical, biblical and theological data are used to illustrate the thesis that the destruction of sin is the result of cooperation between God, the penitent, and the Church. The second part of the book stresses human solidarity in sin.

SHEERIN, JOHN BASIL, C.S.P. *The sacrament of freedom.* Milwaukee: Bruce, 1961. Pp. ix+166. $3.50.

As the title hints, the approach is positive, for the sacrament of penance is looked upon not merely as freedom from sin, but also as freedom for the love of God. Written chiefly for penitents; but those who instruct penitents can also derive much fruit from this book.

SPEYR, ADRIENNE VON. *Confession, the encounter with Christ in penance.* New York: Herder and Herder, 1964. $4.75.

This is a non-technical treatment on penance which opens up the personal dimension of the sacrament and relates it to the theology of the Trinity and the mission of Christ. A useful book for every penitent and confessor.

d) The Eucharist

DELORME, JEAN, and others. *The Eucharist in the New Testament;* a symposium. Baltimore, Md.: (Helicon) Taplinger, 1964. Pp. 160. $3.50.

First published in a special issue of *Lumière et Vie* in 1957. The five essays which comprise this work are written by recognized authorities in NT studies: J. Delorme, P. Benoit, M. E. Boismard, J. Dupont, and D. Mollat. Obviously the reader will not find anything startlingly new about the doctrine of the Eucharist, but the explanations found here present a theological dimension which facilitates a deeper appreciation of this great gift.

FLOOD, EDMUND, O.S.B. *In memory of me.* New York: Sheed and Ward, 1963. Pp. 117. $3.00.

The author reconstructs the institution of the Eucharist at the Last Supper and traces its development down through the centuries to the present day. He does this in a truly scholarly way, using the latest biblical and liturgical findings. In the course of the work he makes criticisms and offers some positive suggestions for reform.

*JORET, FERDINAND D., O.P. *The Eucharist and the confessional.* Westminster, Md.: Newman Press, 1955. Pp. xxx+192. $3.50.

Father Joret conveys his own profound understanding of the sacraments into terms that impart new realizations to his readers, lend new persuasiveness to old truths. Within the rigid framework of the Church's teachings, he develops explanations which tend to enkindle the heart to an adherence to Christ as the source of sanctity. There is one chapter on the sacraments in general, one on the Eucharist and finally, one on the sacrament of penance.

MARTIMORT, AIMÉ GEORGES. *In remembrance of me;* the prayer of the Church and the sacraments. Collegeville, Minn.: Liturgical Press, 1959. Pp. 217. $3.25.

The spirit of the liturgy animates this work. It presents the Church's teaching on the Mass and the sacraments in a new way: the Church and her sacramental system are both life, and a way of life.

*MASURE, EUGENE. *The Christian sacrifice.* New York: P. J. Kenedy, 1943. Pp. 288. $2.25.

Of the many books on the Mass, this is one of the most readable and inspiring. The work is in three parts, treating sacrifice in general, the sacrifice of the Son of God, and the sacrifice of the Mass. The content of the work is sound, but now a little dated as a result of some theological advances made in the past twenty years.

NICHOLAS, MARIE-JOSEPH, O.P. *What is the Eucharist?* Translated by R. F. Trevett. New York: Hawthorn Books, 1960. Pp. 125. $3.50. (Twentieth century encyclopedia of Catholicism, 52)

The author gives a broad overview of his subject. The book is divided into three parts: the Church's faith in the Eucharist, the theology of the Eucharist, and the Eucharistic practice of the Church.

*VAN ACKEN, BERNHARD. *The Holy Eucharist;* the mystery of faith and the sacrament of love. Translated by G. G. Strauss. Westminster, Md.: Newman Press, 1958. Pp. 141. $2.50.

In 1948 the late Cardinal Suhard asked a group of French priests to revitalize the parish of St. Severin in Paris. Their approach was through Eucharistic liturgy, and the effects are reported in this small volume. It can give insight into the liturgical reforms which we are presently implementing.

VONIER, ANSCAR, O.S.B. *A key to the doctrine of the Eucharist.* Westminster, Md.: Newman Press, 1956. Pp. xv+269. $2.75.

Most people know that the Eucharist is a sacrament and a sacrifice, but not many can express the relationship between sacrament and sacrifice. With his clear exposition of the teaching of St. Thomas, Abbot Vonier was perhaps the first in modern times to really understand the fully sacramental character of the Mass.

e) Marriage

ARNOLD, FRANCIS XAVIER. *Woman and man;* their nature and mission. Translated by R. Brennan. New York: Herder and Herder, 1963. Pp. 151. $3.95.

This is one of the best books on the role of woman in today's world. The author is also speaking to men—especially priests.

BURKE, THOMAS W. *The gold ring;* God's pattern for perfect marriage. New York: McKay, 1963. Pp. xv+176. $3.95.

This work was originally a series of articles on "God's pattern for perfect marriage." In 13 chapters the author discusses some of the basic Catholic thinking on the nature of matrimony and its actual fulfillment in married life. The work abounds with fresh insights and deep theology.

*CAFFAREL, HENRI. *Love and grace in marriage.* Translated by F. J. Crosson. Notre Dame, Ind.: Fides Publishers, 1960. Pp. 178. $3.25.

This is not an abstract, theoretical consideration of marriage, but a sound, practical consideration of such problems as the vocation of conjugal love, difficulties in the home, an unfaithful spouse, and others.

_____, ed. *Marriage is holy.* Translated by B. G. Murchland, C.S.C. Chicago: Fides Publishers, 1957. Pp. 219. $1.25.

This is a series of essays by various authors who attempt to touch the inner source of the vitality and sanctity of the married state. The subjects treated are not presented as problems to be solved but as topics for meditation, in the light of the spiritual implications of the vocation of marriage.

KERNS, JOSEPH E., S.J. *The theology of marriage.* New York: Sheed and Ward, 1964. Pp. xiv+302. $6.00.

Isolating a subject is often a help in studying it more closely. This is precisely what the author has done. He focuses on just one aspect of married life, the effort which the spouses make to improve each other. His approach is concrete, realistic, and up-to-date.

LECLERCQ, JACQUES. *Marriage, a great sacrament.* 3rd ed. Dublin: Cahill, 1962. Pp. 172. $1.95.

This volume presents the ideal of Christian marriage in all its fullness and candor, the candor spoken of in the Church's nuptial blessing. It presents an ideal of conjugal spirituality which may prove to be one of the great developments of the Catholic life of our time.

LESTAPIS, STANISLAS DE, S.J. *Family planning and modern problems.* Translated by R. F. Trevett. New York: Herder and Herder, 1961. Pp. 326. $6.50. Pap. $1.25.

Until this book was translated from the French there was nothing of its type in English. Part I: a historic survey of family planning. Part II: a critical assessment of the use of contraceptives. Part III: the Catholic position. Part IV: the Catholic's mission in the world.

*MIHANOVICH, CLEMENT S. and WERTH, ALVIN, O.F.M. Cap. *Papal pronouncements on marriage and the family.* Milwaukee: Bruce, 1955. Pp. xiii+189. $3.00.

The popes do not normally exercise their infallible teaching office in encyclicals, allocutions, and addresses. Nevertheless, Catholics look with respect to their contents. Here in one volume we have the papal pronouncements made during the past 75 years on the subject of marriage and the family. The contents are grouped under appropriate headings.

MIHANOVICH, CLEMENT S., and others. *Guide to Catholic marriage.* Rev. ed. Milwaukee: Bruce, 1963. Pp. 344. $4.50.

A one-volume library of information on all the important aspects of marriage: spiritual, legal, psychological, physical and financial. The work contains little on the new approach of psychological fulfillment, but it is certainly worthwhile reading for anyone concerned with marriage.

NEWLAND, MARY R. *We and our children.* New York: P. J. Kenedy, 1954. Pp. 271. $3.95. Pap. Image (D123) $0.85.

There is nothing sentimental or pietistic about this mother's approach to raising a family in the fear of God. Christian parenthood is treated simply as a matter of concrete decisions which flow from the Gospels and the teachings of the Church.

*O'MAHONY, PATRICK J., ed. *Catholics and divorce.* New York: T. Nelson, 1959. Pp. ix+116. $2.95.

To give "a clear and concise statement of the Catholic viewpoint" is the expressed purpose of this collection of seven articles on marriage and divorce. The only moderate success of the work is perhaps to be attributed to its wide scope; sweeping generalizations weaken its appeal. However, the book is useful and informative in spite of some of these shortcomings.

*ORAISON, MARC. *Union in marital love;* its physical and spiritual foundations. Translated by A. Humbert. New York: Macmillan, 1958. Pp. vii+ 129. $3.00.

While Catholic couples usually know the precepts of Christian morality in marriage, they are frequently unaware of the biological, psychological and theological data which the law takes for granted. The purpose of this book is to dispel some of this ignorance. A very useful work for anyone contemplating marriage, or for anyone who does marriage counseling.

SCHLECK, CHARLES A. *The sacrament of matrimony:* a dogmatic study. Milwaukee: Bruce, 1964. Pp. xii+290. $5.00.

This book is an attempt to start work in the direction of a dogmatic approach to the sacrament of marriage. It combines the more traditional approach to the sacrament with the new approach. In doing so it cites recent papal documents, particularly as these touch the primacy of procreation in regard to the hierarchy of marriage values.

SUENENS, LEON JOSEPH CARDINAL. *Love and control.* Translated by G. Robinson. Westminster, Md.: Newman Press, 1961. Pp. 200. $3.25. Pap. $0.95.

The problems of the increasing population, personal poverty in families, and the regulation of births are given a clear expression in the framework of a Catholic conscience. It does not remain on the level of the theoretical, but gets to practical solutions.

THOMAS, JOHN L., S. J. *The Catholic viewpoint on marriage.* New York: Hanover, 1958. Pp. 192. $3.50.

The Church's teaching on courtship, marriage, sex, birth control and divorce stands unalterably opposed to a philosophy of comfort, convenience and concupiscence. It has been the goal of this author to present an understandable exposition of the Church's doctrine in these controversial areas.

*WILKIN, VINCENT, S.J. *The image of God in sex.* New York: Sheed and Ward, 1955. Pp. 88. $1.75.

The author mildly shocks the reader into an appreciation of the holiness of sex. He does so by showing how sex flows from the perfect mystery of generation where the Father is Himself an eternal act of generation.

f) Holy Orders

*BLIGH, JOHN, S.J. *Ordination to the priesthood.* New York: Sheed and Ward, 1955. Pp. xv+189. $3.00.

In his preface the author writes that this is not a pious meditation on the priesthood, but a liturgical and theological essay, written in the belief that a careful analysis of the rite will in the end be more conducive to solid piety than a devotional treatment on the subject. Truly an excellent commentary on the ordination rite.

LÉCUYER, JOSEPH. *What is a priest?* New York: Hawthorn Books, 1959. Pp. 125. $3.50. (Twentieth century encyclopedia of Catholicism, 53)

One of the best volumes in the series, a small masterpiece in which the author discusses the priesthood of the apostles, the nature of the episcopate, the priesthood and the diaconate. His treatment of the priesthood of the laity is especially good, and timely.

McGOWAN, JEAN C., R.S.C.J. *Concelebration:* sign of the unity of the Church. New York: Herder and Herder, 1964. Pp. xxiii+128. $3.75.

Mother McGowan gives a brief history of concelebration with special emphasis on the current practice in the Western Church, and reviews recent dogmatic discussion associated with the subject. It is presumed that those who are interested in reading about concelebration will bring with them some theological background. Unless they do, there might be some misun derstanding by the reader.

MOSSHAMER, OTTILIE. *The priest and womanhood.* Translated by R. J Voight. Baltimore, Md.: Newman Press, 1964. Pp. 388. $5.75.

The author was commissioned to write this study by the Pontifical Insti tute for Priestly Vocations. It is an attempt to explain to women what it i to be a priest, and to priests what it is to be a woman. The relevance of the book is that it can show how both might cooperate in furthering God' kingdom on earth.

*SPICQ, CESLAUS, O.P. *The mystery of Godliness.* Translated by J. Martin Chicago: Fides Publishers, 1954. Pp. 183. $3.50.

The French title gives a more accurate picture of the contents of thi book. It is a scriptural theology of priestly life, based on the epistles to Tim othy and Titus.

*STOCKUMS, WILHELM. *The priesthood.* St. Louis, Mo.: B. Herder Book Co., 1942. Pp. 241. $1.75.

In scholarly but lucid style the author discusses the nature of the priest hood, and the priesthood in its relation to the Church, the people, the world at large and to the priest himself. While the author is presenting an ideal he remains a realist. Although this book was written more than 20 years ago, his sympathetic insights are still pertinent to the perennial and current problems of the ministry.

VEUILLOT, PIERRE, ed. *The Catholic priesthood according to the teaching of the Church:* papal documents from Pius X to Pius XII. [See page 92.]

g) The Last Anointing

DIDIER, JEAN CHARLES. *Death and the Christian.* New York: Hawthorn Books, 1961. Pp. 157. $3.50. (Twentieth century encyclopedia of Catholi cism, 55)

The author's aim was to furnish an accurate and stimulating apprecia tion of the place of Christ's healing action in the life of the Christian. Throughout, he maintains an awareness that the whole man, body as well as soul, is the subject of redemption. This is a masterful condensation of a wealth of theological data on the subject.

F. THE THEOLOGY OF THE CHURCH

ADAM, KARL. *The spirit of Catholicism.* Translated by J. McCann, O.S.B. Garden City, N.Y.: Doubleday, 1959. Pp. 288. Pap. Image (D2) $0.85.

Although first published in 1929, this classic on ecclesiology has lost nothing of its stature. The author understands the Church primarily as a community, a community made up of persons in need of redemption, a community whose unity is established in the person of the incarnate Son of God.

*BERRIGAN, DANIEL. *The Bride;* essays in the Church. New York: Mac millan, 1959. Pp. 142. $3.50.

The author is convinced that men of faith have been willing to let their lives speak for their beliefs while heresies and untruths continue to go un challenged. With an economy of words he presents some thought-provok ing insights into historiography and the nature of salvation history.

BULLOUGH, SEBASTIAN, O.P. *Roman Catholicism.* Baltimore, Md.: Penguin Books, 1964. Pp. 330. Pap. $1.25.

The author presents us with an integrated portrait of Roman Catholicism and shows that its main tenets are both reasonable and consistent.

BURTNESS, JAMES H. and KILDAHL, JOHN P. edd. *The new community in Christ;* essays on the corporate Christian life. Minneapolis, Minn.: Augsburg Publishing House, 1963. Pp. 207. $4.50.

This is a compilation of nine essays on the Church, by nine Lutheran theologians. Their concern is not to sharpen the peculiarities of the Lutheran tradition over against the rest of Christendom, but to consider problems and objectives that involve all Churches that confess Jesus Christ. Catholics will benefit much by reading it.

BUTLER, CHRISTOPHER, O.S.B. *The idea of the Church.* Baltimore, Md.: (Helicon) Taplinger, 1963. Pp. xi+236. $4.95.

The character of this book is more apologetic than ecumenical or scriptural. Yet it is apologetics at its best because its arguments are based on up-dated history, scripture, and ecumenics.

CHADWICK, OWEN. *From Bossuet to Newman:* the idea of doctrinal development. New York: Cambridge University Press, 1957. Pp. x+249. $5.50.

The author writes from an Anglican viewpoint. The Catholic theologian may at times utter a mild demurrer, but the historian will be delighted at its objectivity, its tone, its wit, and its masterful scholarship.

THE CHURCH; readings in theology. Compiled at the Canisianum, Innsbruck. New York: P. J. Kenedy, 1963. Pp. 242. $4.95.

This is a compilation and translation of fourteen essays on the Church by leading Catholic theologians. Some of the contributors are Hugo and Karl Rahner, R. Guardini, J. Jungmann, S. Lyonnet, and H. Küng. The book contains three parts: the first deals with the fundamental truths about the Church in her essence and structure, the second with the openness of the Church to the problems of mankind, and the third with reflections centering directly on the Church in Council.

CONGAR, YVES, O.P. *The mystery of the Church.* Translated by A. V. Littledale. Baltimore, Md.: (Helicon) Taplinger, 1960. Pp. 260. $4.75.

This book unites two other works by the author which were originally published in French. The first part is an informal series of talks given to pilgrims traveling to Chartres for Pentecost; the second part is a series of more learned treatises on the unity of the Church.

GUITTON, JEAN. *The Church and the Gospel.* Translated by E. Craufurd. Chicago: H. Regnery, 1961. Pp. 288. $6.50.

Although not concerned with polemics, this book meets the challenge of the question, "What is the relationship between Jesus and the Church?" The author concludes that the key to understanding the Church is a comprehension of the full import of the Incarnation. The autobiographical form of this book contributes to its readability.

HAMER, JEROME, O.P. *The Church is a communion.* New York: Sheed and Ward, 1965. Pp. 240. $5.00.

This is a theological investigation beginning with an historical survey of the emergence of the term "mystical body" to describe the Church in the years between the First Vatican Council and *Mystici Corporis.* As such, this book throws light on a subject which has always been with us, but which had faded from the attention of Catholic theologians.

HASSEVELDT, ROGER. *The Church, a divine mystery.* Translated by W. Storey. Chicago: Fides Publishers, 1954. Pp. xii+263. $4.50.

The author has set out to make an appraisal of the Church from within and attempts an exposition of its organic aspect. He approaches his subject through what he calls the three phases of the Church: past, present and future. The biblical and patristic sources which the author cites are a real service to the reader.

*JOHNSTON, GEORGE. *The doctrine of the Church in the New Testament.* New York: Macmillan, 1943. Pp. xvi+156. $2.50.

The author shows that the early Church was "not merely an organization or institution," but is less successful in his attempt to prove that the primitive Church did not consider itself an organization.

*KIRK, KENNETH E., ed. *The apostolic ministry.* London: Hodder and Stoughton, 1947. Pp. xiv+573. $7.50.

Subtitle: a series of essays by ten experts on the history and doctrine of the episcopacy. The study was made by Anglicans and has stimulated great discussion and the interest of both Anglicans and Roman Catholics.

KNOX, JOHN. *The early Church and the coming great Church.* Nashville, Tenn.: Abingdon Press, 1955. Pp. 160. $2.50.

The author finds a remarkable resemblance between the early Church and the Church today.

KÜNG, HANS. *Structures of the Church.* New York: T. Nelson, 1964. Pp. xviii+394. $7.50.

This is a further development of considerations similar to those expressed in the *Council, Reform, and Reunion,* by the same author. An interesting quality of Father Küng's investigations is that he disqualifies no questions. He intrepidly tackles such problems as: Must all valid Councils be convoked by the pope? Can the pope define a doctrine infallibly without the Church? May and should laymen take part in a Council with full voting rights?

*LOCHET, LOUIS. *Son of the Church.* Translated by A. J. La Mothe. Chicago: Fides Publishers, 1956. Pp. xiii+255. $4.50.

This book is a thoughtful review of the work of the Church as the continuation of Christ's redemptive act. The personal element enters into this study insofar as the author makes a self-examination of his attitudes, intentions, and activities to see if they are in harmony with the Church.

LUBAC, HENRI DE, S.J. *The Catholic and his Church.* Translated by M. Mason. New York: Sheed and Ward, 1960. Pp. 90. $0.75.

This is an abridgement of the author's more comprehensive work, *The Splendor of the Church.* Partial contents: Catholic solidarity; Catholic obedience; Catholic security; Sterile criticizing; Applying the wrong standards; Spiritual superiority.

————. *The splendor of the Church.* Translated by M. Mason. Glen Rock, N. J.: Paulist Press, 1956. Pp. 352. Pap. $1.25.

It would be difficult to name other theologians who have written on the Church as the Mystical Body of Christ with equal success. This work touches on so many points that it is virtually a brief compendium of theology. The wisdom and erudition of the author are stimulating and enriching.

MACKEY, JAMES PATRICK. *The modern theology of tradition.* New York: Herder and Herder, 1963. Pp. xi+219. $4.95.

It has been said that this is the most serviceable Catholic monograph on the subject. Father Mackey associates himself with those who hold that in addition to hierarchical pronouncements, the witness of theologians and the *sensus fidelium* have their own value as a source of tradition.

*MONTCHEUIL, YVES DE, S.J. *Aspects of the Church.* Translated by A. J. LaMothe. Chicago: Fides Publishers, 1955. Pp. 197. $3.75.

Not a difficult book, but rather a lucid and engrossing one, written simply and clearly with erudition, sobriety of thought and logical reasoning. The author is completely honest in that he shuns no issues, nor glosses over contradictions; but rather he points up negative comments and attacks made upon the Church from outside.

MOODY, JOSEPH NESTOR, ed. *Church and society.* New York: Arts, inc., 1953. Pp. 914. $12.00.

Here we have a one-volume work which presents the history of Catholic social and political thought since the end of the 18th century. Both editor and contributors show good judgment in evaluating social and political thought movements. Documents accompany most chapters.

NORRIS, FRANK B., S.S. *God's own people;* an introductory study of the Church. Baltimore, Md.: (Helicon) Taplinger, 1962. Pp. v+122. $2.95.

This work serves as a bridge between the scholar and the general reader. The Church is considered in no narrow sense, but in the sweep of sacred history. With such a broad canvas to paint, certain areas are not given a very detailed treatment, but the book gives a good comprehensive overview.

PERRIN, NORMAN. *The kingdom of God in the teaching of Jesus.* Philadelphia: Westminster Press, 1963. Pp. 215. $4.50.

Schleiermacher, Schweitzer, Dodd, Manson, Bultmann, Cullmann — these are only a few of the men considered as the author presents a historical survey of the concept of the kingdom. This is a valuable one-volume compendium of Protestant theology on the Church.

RAHNER, KARL, S.J. *The Church and the sacraments.* Translated by W. J. O'Hara. New York: Herder and Herder, 1963. Pp. 117. $2.25.

The Church is described as the continuation of Christ's presence in the world, and thus the fundamental sacrament. The implications of this view are quite astounding; among other things it becomes apparent that each of the sacraments in its specific structure flows of necessity from the fundamental nature of the Church.

SCHARP, HENRICH. *How the Catholic Church is governed.* New York: Herder and Herder, 1960. Pp. 168. $2.95. Pap. Paulist Press, $0.75.

The author is a German newspaperman who spent many years as a correspondent in Rome. He wrote this book for his countrymen with the intention of sharing with them his observations and experiences. He presents a good general sketch of the complexities in the administration of the vast organization that the Church is.

SCHEPERS, MAURICE BONAVENTURE, O.P. *The Church of Christ.* Englewood Cliffs, N. J.: Prentice-Hall, 1963. Pp. 118. $3.95. Pap. $1.50.

Before all else, the author considers him who brought the Church into being, him to whom the Church is going, and him to whose image the Church is conformed: Christ. The reader will be able to penetrate more deeply into the mystery of the Church after he has read these profound thoughts on the subject.

VOS, GEERHARDUS. *The teaching of Jesus concerning the kingdom and the Church*. Grand Rapids, Mich.: Eerdmans Publishing Co., 1958. Pp. 103. $2.00.

Because of the prominence given to the notion of the kingdom of God in the synoptic Gospels, the author sets out to delineate the nature of this kingdom in three successive chapters, each entitled, "The Essence of the Kingdom." These constitute the middle half of the book; the introductory and concluding chapters go to make a good coherent study.

G. THE THEOLOGY OF MARY

BERNARD, ROGATIANUS, O.P. *The mystery of Mary*. Translated by A. Bouchard. St. Louis, Mo.: B. Herder Book Co., 1960. Pp. xv+304. $4.95.

This book concerns itself with Our Lady's spiritual maternity, her motherhood of grace, through which she comes to be called the Mother of all Christians. The treatment is more devotional than theological, however.

BOUYER, LOUIS, C.Or. *Seat of Wisdom;* an essay on the place of the Virgin Mary in Christian theology. Translated by A. V. Littledale. New York: Pantheon Books, 1962. Pp. ix+212. $4.50.

The author first treats of the scriptural themes of Mariology, then devotes a chapter to Mary in the NT, and in the rest of the book carefully examines the place of Mary in theology. The work reflects the author's familiarity with the Fathers and his theological insights.

DEHAU, PETER THOMAS, O.P. *Eve and Mary*. Translated by the Dominican Nuns of the Perpetual Rosary. St. Louis, Mo.: B. Herder Book Co., 1958. Pp. ix+268. $3.95.

Drawing chiefly on sacred scripture and St. Thomas, the author contrasts the influence of Eve on mankind with that of Mary. He achieves profundity without obscurity, thoroughness without pedantry, and piety without sickening sweetness.

*DOHENY, WILLIAM JOSEPH and KELLY, JOSEPH P. *Papal documents on Mary*. Milwaukee: Bruce, 1954. Pp. x+270. $4.50.

The most important papal documents issued in the last 100 years are gathered in this volume. It is a compendium of sound Marian theology, a necessary basis for sound Marian devotion.

GALOT, JEAN, S.J. *Mary in the Gospel*. Translated by Sister Maria Constance, S.C.H. Westminster, Md.: Newman Press, 1964. Pp. 230. $3.95.

The aim of this book is to sketch an initial Marian theology from selected passages in the Gospels in which Mary is mentioned. The literal sense of the texts is examined first, and only then is there an attempt to arrive at a fuller sense.

GAROFALO, SALVATORE. *Mary in the Bible*. Translated by T. J. Tobin. Milwaukee: Bruce, 1961. Pp. 106. $3.00.

The author discusses the role of Mary as recorded in scripture, beginning with the Annunciation, and concluding with the Woman clothed with the sun, in the Apocalypse.

*NEWMAN, JOHN HENRY CARDINAL. *The new Eve*. Westminster, Md.: Newman Press, 1952. Pp. 96. $0.60.

This little book is an excerpt from the author's writings on Roman Catholic belief about the Blessed Virgin Mary. It presents the traditional and universal teaching of the Gospels and the Fathers on Our Lady. Its sober approach has nothing in common with the emotional veneration stimulated by such phenomena as apparitions and cures.

O'CONNOR, EDWARD DENIS, C.S.C., ed. *The dogma of the Immaculate Conception:* history and significance. Notre Dame, Ind.: University of Notre Dame Press, 1958. Pp. xviii+665. $10.00.

In its conception this work seems intended to be as broad and deep a study of the Immaculate Conception as is possible at the present time. It is a symposium drawing from European, Canadian, and American scholarship.

_____. *The mystery of Woman.* Notre Dame, Ind.: University of Notre Dame Press, 1956. Pp. x+150. $2.75.

This book is composed of three outstanding essays which examine the theological significance of Mary's supernatural privileges: the divine motherhood, the Immaculate Conception, and the Assumption. One would be hard put to find another scholarly work cast in such well-chosen phrases.

RAHNER, KARL, S.J. *Mary, Mother of the Lord.* Translated by W. J. O'Hara. New York: Herder and Herder, 1963. Pp. 107. $2.95.

This book contains eight conferences given at the University Church of the Holy Trinity in Innsbruck during May devotions. Were it not for the reputation of the author, we might expect to find in it something quite different from what it actually contains. However, these are undoubtedly the most solidly theological May devotion conferences on the Blessed Virgin Mary that have ever been given.

*SHEEBEN, MATHIAS JOSEPH. *Mariology.* 2v. Translated by T. L. M. J. Geukers. St. Louis, Mo.: B. Herder Book Co., 1947. $3.00 each.

Besides the solid core of Marian theology which is presented in this work, an interesting sidelight for the serious and informed general reader is the author's distinction between solid theology and pious legends which shows that while the Church's dogmatic definitions are dependent on the former, the latter are not always wholly misguided.

SCHILLEBEECKX, EDWARD, O.P. *Mary, Mother of the redemption.* New York: Sheed and Ward, 1964. Pp. 191. $4.50.

Having made his mark with the publication of *Christ, the sacrament of the encounter with God,* the eminent Dutch theologian now turns his mind and talent to a consideration of the Church's teaching on Mary. This is an easier book to read than the one on the sacraments. What the author has to say is enlightening and especially timely.

SEMMELROTH, OTTO, S. J. *Mary, archetype of the Church.* New York: Sheed and Ward, 1963. Pp. xiv+175. $3.95.

Jaroslav Pelikan's introduction points up the ecumenical importance of Mary for understanding Christ in the Church. The author attempts to situate Mary in the economy of salvation as coredemptrix and mediatrix.

SUENENS, LEON JOSEPH CARDINAL. *Mary the mother of God.* Translated by Sister Anselma Brennel. New York: Hawthorn Books, 1959. Pp. 139. $3.50. (Twentieth century encyclopedia of Catholicism, 44)

This book combines theological depth with popular presentation. There is a fine chapter on Mary in the divine plan. Other chapters treat of the Immaculate Conception, the Annunciation, the Incarnation, the redemption, and the Motherhood of Mary and the Church.

THURIAN, MAX. *Mary, Mother of all Christians.* New York: Herder and
Herder, 1964. Pp. 204. $4.75.

A superb example of biblical theology from which the author derives his
thought on Mary's virginity, her divine motherhood, her place in the Church
and as a type of the Church. He makes some references to patristic sources
and although he quotes the Reformers, it would be difficult to find a single
concept that a Catholic could not accept with enthusiasm.

H. THE THEOLOGY OF DEATH AND THE LAST THINGS

BOURGY, PAUL, O.P. *The resurrection of Christ and of Christians.* Translated by R. E. Marieb, O. P. Dubuque, Ia.: Priory Press, 1963. Pp. 88.
Pap. $0.95.

This is a summary of the Easter mystery. It begins with sin and its consequences of suffering and death; next there is a consideration of the Incarnation and the redemptive death of Christ, the resurrection; and finally the
last days and their consummation in the Second Coming of Christ are treated.

*CERFAUX, LUCIEN. *Christ in the theology of St. Paul.* [See page 27.]

CULLMANN, OSCAR. *Christ and time;* the primitive Christian conception
of time and history. Rev. ed. Translated by F. Filson. Philadelphia: Westminster Press, 1964. Pp. 253. $5.50.

The discussion which the publication of this book evoked is evidence that
the author deals in a scholarly and vital way with an issue central to biblical
study and Christian theology. His views on redemptive history are worth
reading for a balanced evaluation of more traditional authors.

DIDIER, JEAN CHARLES. *Death and the Christian.* Translated by P. J.
Hepburne-Scott. New York: Hawthorn Books, 1961. Pp. 106. $3.50.
(Twentieth century encyclopedia of Catholicism, 55)

The first six chapters provide extremely interesting historical background.
Beginning with the seventh chapter, "Danger of Death," the author discusses doctrinal concepts, his forte.

DURRWELL, FRANCIS XAVIER, C.SS.R. *In the redeeming Christ.* [See
page 27.]

_____. *The resurrection.* [See page 27.]

DYER, GEORGE J. *Limbo: unsettled question.* New York: Sheed and Ward,
1964. Pp. xii+196. $3.95.

The author traces the main lines of the history of theological thinking
regarding the existence of limbo and the fate of unbaptized infants, from
the patristic period to modern times. Although this work is an adaptation
of a doctoral thesis, it is easy to read and is worthy of the attention of priests
and students of theology.

GLEASON, ROBERT W., S.J. *The world to come.* New York: Sheed and
Ward, 1962. Pp. 172. $3.95. Pap. $2.25.

Although the book is neither technical nor scientific in its message, there
can be no doubt that the author is thoroughly familiar with the tradition
and current theology of the subject under discussion. He has selected the
best of this, and put it into readable form.

*GUARDINI, ROMANO. *The last things.* Translated by C. Forsyth and G.
Granham. New York: Pantheon, 1954. Pp. 118. $2.75.

This is a series of provocative essays on certain aspects of doctrines proper to eschatology. By admission, therefore, it is incomplete. It evidences both the enthusiasm of a scholar and the detachment of a mystic.

RAHNER, KARL, S.J. *On the theology of death.* Translated by C. Henkey. New York: Herder and Herder, 1961. Pp. 127. $2.25. (Quaestiones disputatae, 2)

Rahner's purpose is to analyze the meaning of death as an event which involves the whole man, as a consequence of sin, and as a sharing in the death of Christ. This approach to a subject of renewed interest is rather unique.

SCHILLEBEECKX, EDWARD, O.P. *Christ the sacrament of the encounter with God.* [See page 39.]

SCHNACKENBURG, RUDOLF. *New Testament thology today.* [See page 29.]

TROISFONTAINES, ROGER, S.J. *I do not die.* Translated by F. E. Albert. New York: Desclee, 1963. Pp. 295. $4.75.

The good death which the author speaks about is the spiritual re-birth of both soul and body. Life is an apprenticeship for death, the true life. The author seems to have been enlightened by the best of recent approaches to perennial truth. He has presented his philosophy as a coherent unity, but demands the reader's reflection for a real penetration of his message.

WINKLHOFER, ALOIS. *The coming of his kingdom:* a theology of the last things. [See page 30.]

III
LITURGY

AMIOT, FRANÇOIS. *History of the Mass.* New York: Hawthorn Books, 1959. Pp. 141. $3.50. (Twentieth century encyclopedia of Catholicism, 110)

The author touches upon the origin, development and interpretation of the Mass ritual as it exists today. From this historical overview one can more readily appraise their true value in the light of the latest discoveries.

ATTWATER, DONALD. *The Christian Churches of the East.* 2d ed. Milwaukee: Bruce, 1962. Pp. 260. $7.50.

This is a revision and an up-dating of the author's popular and accurate description of the Christian Churches not in communion with Rome. Its appendices, indexes and glossary make it a usable compendium for information on Eastern Christianity.

BOUYER, LOUIS, C.Or. *Rite and man:* natural sacredness and Christian liturgy. Translated by M. J. Costelloe. Notre Dame, Ind.: University of Notre Dame Press, 1963. Pp. 220. $6.00. (Liturgical studies, 7)

An attempt to provide a better understanding of Christian ritual. While the author views his work as a survey to be made obsolete by more penetrating studies, it is the consensus of many reviewers that this book is not likely to be surpassed in the near future. Not everyone will agree with all of the author's observations, but surely one must admit the value of seeking a foundation of the supernatural in the natural. After reading this book, one can see why a technical course in theology today can begin with a study of the sacraments.

BRASO, GABRIEL M., O.S.B. *Liturgy and spirituality.* Collegeville, Minn.: Liturgical Press, 1960. Pp. xii+247. $3.50

To single out such obstacles to liturgical renewal as individualism, superficiality, and utilitarianism is not new. Nor is the author the first to discuss other pertinent subjects like concelebration. This book, however, is distinguished by a theological depth and breadth coupled with sobriety.

BRIDGE, ANTHONY CYPRIAN. *Images of God:* an essay on the life and death of symbols. London: Hodder and Stoughton, 1960. Pp. 158. $2.25.

Having defined symbolism as the meeting of sensitive phenomena with immaterial and transcendent realities, the author establishes a parallel between works of art and the expression of Christian faith. He suggests a new method for the presentation of the Christian message by going back to the use of symbols.

CASEL, ODO, O.S.B. *The mystery of Christian worship and other writings.* Translated and edited by B. Neunheuser, O.S.B. Westminster, Md.: Newman Press, 1962. Pp. xvii+212. $5.75.

A translation of Casel's controversial *Das christliche Kult-mysterium* and other writings, in which he elaborates his mystery-presence theory regarding the liturgy. The author's thought is more discursive and intuitive than one is used to finding in the writings of professional theologians.

CRICHTON, JOHN D. *The Church's worship.* New York: Sheed and Ward, 1964. Pp. 246. $5.00.

A book-length consideration of the *Constitution on the Sacred Liturgy,* with a lucid explanation of the theology behind it.

DALMAIS, IRENEE H. *Introduction to the liturgy.* Translated by R. Capel. Baltimore, Md.: (Helicon) Taplinger, 1961. Pp. ix +194. $4.50.

The greater part of this book is devoted to a theological analysis of Christian worship. It will help the reader to penetrate the inner reality of the liturgy, giving him a clear and accurate review of the liturgy in its historical, sacramental and sociological aspects.

DAVIS, CHARLES. *Liturgy and doctrine;* the doctrinal basis of the liturgical movement. New York: Sheed and Ward, 1961. Pp. 123. $2.50.

The only adverse criticism of this book has been that it is too short. The author sketches the nature of the liturgical movement and proceeds to dwell briefly on some of the major themes of Christian doctrine such as the sacraments, the risen Christ, history of salvation, liturgy and mystery, sacrifice and eschatology.

DELORME, JEAN, and others. *The Eucharist in the New Testament;* a symposium. [See page 42.]

DIEKMANN, GODFREY, O.S.B. *Come, let us worship.* Baltimore, Md.: (Helicon) Taplinger, 1961. Pp. 180. $4.50.

This is a collection of papers delivered at various National Liturgical Conferences from 1940 to 1960. They came from the pen of a pioneer in the American liturgical movement and articulate many of the desires for reform which are being implemented in the current liturgical renewal.

DIGGES, MARY LAURENTIA, C.S.J. *Transfigured world;* design, theme and symbol in worship. New York: Farrar, Straus and Cudahy, 1957. Pp. xvi+240. $4.00.

The author discusses the transfiguration of nature that takes place in the liturgy. The hours of the day and seasons of the year become instruments of grace.

GELINEAU, JOSEPH, S.J. *Voices and instruments in Christian worship.* Translated by C. Howell. Collegeville, Minn.: Liturgical Press, 1964. Pp. 224. $4.00.

When this book first appeared in French in 1962 it was the first contemporary synthesis of scholarship in both the liturgy and its music. The book will aid the pastor and the parish musician in a better understanding of how to buy and what to plan, to make sure that the new format of the liturgy will be a natural and worthy successor to the best of its ancestry.

JENNY, HENRI. *The paschal mystery in the Christian year.* Translated by A. Stehling and J. Lundberg. Notre Dame, Ind.: Fides Publishers, 1962. Pp. 112. Pap. $1.50.

Because of its outline form, this book is not recommended for reading straight through. It was written originally to aid teachers in presenting the Church year in terms of the paschal mystery. It can also provide preachers with this same orientation.

JUNGMANN, JOSEF A., S.J. *The early liturgy to the time of Gregory the Great.* Translated by F. A. Brunner, C.SS.R. Notre Dame, Ind.: University of Notre Dame Press, 1959. Pp. 314. $6.00. (Liturgical studies, 6)

A renowned liturgical scholar examines the worship of the primitive

Church. Later chapters investigate the development of the liturgy from the time of the apologists to Gregory the Great.

_____. *The Eucharistic prayer;* a study of the *Canon Missae.* Translated by R. L. Batley. Notre Dame, Ind.: Fides Publishers, 1956. Pp. 55. $0.75.

This excellent summary presents a theological exposition of the Mass, a concise analysis of its historical developments, and serves as a guide to selective principles likely to govern future reforms. The material was first presented by the author at a liturgical conference for priests.

_____. *The Mass of the Roman rite.* 2v. Translated by F. A. Brunner, C.SS.R. New York: Benziger, 1951 and 1955. $9.25 each. One-volume ed., abridged and edited by C. K. Riepe, 1959. $10.00.

Immediately after publication, this work became definitive for the history of the Roman Mass. The one-volume work provides a more direct account, without the wealth of detail and bibliographical apparatus.

_____. *Pastoral liturgy.* New York: Herder and Herder, 1962. Pp. 430. $6.95.

This is an excellent translation of the original German work, *Liturgisches Erbe und Pastorale Gegenwart.* The author realizes that the liturgy is by nature conservative, but he is also realistic in pointing out some concrete problems which clamor for solution through adaptation.

_____. *Public worship;* a survey. Translated by C. Howell, S.J. Collegeville, Minn.: Liturgical Press, 1958. Pp. vii+249. $3.50.

In three years this book was published in four different languages. In his preface the author says, "I have taken the opportunity of summarizing and setting in order the most important elements of the lectures I have been wont to deliver to young theologians during the last three decades." It is a masterpiece in miniature; no page is without surprise. For priests the chapter on the divine office will take on special significance.

LIESEL, NIKOLAUS. *The Eucharistic liturgies of the Eastern Churches.* Collegeville, Minn.: Liturgical Press, 1963. Pp. 310. $8.00.

More than 800 photographs present the significant gestures of the 12 most noteworthy non-Latin Rites. This work also provides a commentary which is accurate and non-technical. An especially helpful feature is a series of maps which designate the principal areas where each rite is predominant.

McGOWAN, JEAN C., R.S.C.J. *Concelebration:* sign of the unity of the Church. [See page 45.]

McMANUS, FREDERICK R., ed. *Revival of the liturgy.* New York: Herder and Herder, 1963. Pp. 224. $4.50.

This is a *festschrift* honoring Father Godfrey Diekmann, O.S.B., for a quarter-century as editor of *Worship.* Because of the work of this liturgical pioneer, cynics no longer smile at the liturgical movement. Father Mc-Manus's book can help to guide others in implementing the mind of the Church in this area.

MARITAIN, JACQUES and MARITAIN, RAISSA. *Liturgy and contemplation.* Translated by J. W. Evans. New York: P. J. Kenedy, 1960. Pp. 96. $2.95.

In this study there is an attempt to show the intimate relationship between liturgy and contemplation, and that neither can be sacrificed to the other. The material originally appeared as articles in the quarterly review, *Spiritual Life.*

MILLER, JOHN H., C.S.C. *Fundamentals of the liturgy*. Notre Dame, Ind.: Fides Publishers, 1960. Pp. 531. $6.00.

Intended as a textbook for seminarians, religious and lay apostles, this work contains a detailed introduction to all the major areas of liturgical theory and practice. The author might have placed a greater emphasis on the sacramental efficacy of the liturgy and used more scripture.

MARTIMORT, AIMÉ GEORGES, ed. *The liturgy and the Word of God*. Collegeville, Minn.: Liturgical Press, 1959. Pp. xv+183. $3.50.

This is a collection of papers given at the Third National Liturgical Congress at Strasbourg, in France, 1958. It exemplifies the emergence of an area of common interest among scholars in the formerly separated fields of liturgical and biblical studies.

_____. *The signs of the new covenant*. [See page 38.]

NOCENT, ADRIAN, O.S.B. *The future of the liturgy*. New York: Herder and Herder, 1963. Pp. 215. $3.95.

The balanced views of the author show him to be a man with both foresight and the caution of one who sees scattered merits in the status quo. He shows tact, but is also frank and specific in reviewing history and making suggestions for the future.

PARSCH, PIUS. *The Church's year of grace*. 5v. Translated by W. Heidt. Collegeville, Minn.: Liturgical Press, 1958. $4.00 each. Pap. $2.75.

Monsignor Martin Hellriegel, an esteemed pioneer of the liturgical movement has suggested that the faithful prepare the Mass text by reading it over the night before, in order that they might derive a deeper share in the riches of the Church's liturgy. In this work of Dr. Parsch we find an additional aid, a guide which will explain and elucidate the text. As a commentary on the Mass texts, it is the best there is in English.

_____. *The liturgy of the Mass*. Rev. ed. Translated by H. E. Winstone. St. Louis: B. Herder Book Co., 1957. Pp. xii+344. $4.95.

The revision incorporates new material gathered through long years of experience. The result is not only a practical manual for introducing the congregation to active participation, but a source book for understanding the basic liturgical themes and an aid in seeing how they have come to be expressed in the form of the liturgy which we have today.

RAHNER, HUGO, S.J. *Greek myths and Christian mystery*. Translated by B. Battershaw. New York: Harper and Row, 1963. Pp. 399. $10.00.

The English reading public now has available a work that has become a classic on the subject. The author steers a middle course between postulating Christianity's complete dependence on mystery cults and denying categorically that there was any influence at all.

REINHOLD, HANS A. *Bringing the Mass to the people*. Baltimore, Md.: (Helicon) Taplinger, 1960. Pp. v+114. $2.95.

Anyone who has ever looked upon the Mass as a dry, formless prayer will gain new horizons after reading this book. The pioneer liturgist and author leads the reader to discover that the Mass is a finely wrought drama which makes Calvary present and enables Christ to worship the Father through his own Mystical Body.

_____. *Dynamics of liturgy*. New York: Macmillan, 1961. Pp. xii+146. $4.75.

The author here treats the beginnings of the liturgical movement and explains the concept of liturgy as the work of the people. He treats the high points of the liturgical year and offers some suggestions for reform.

ROGUET, AIMO M., O.P. *Holy Mass:* approaches to the mystery. Translated by Carisbrooke Dominicans. Collegeville, Minn.: Liturgical Press, 1953. Pp. 120. $1.10.

The author's purpose is not only to talk about the Mass, but to encourage each Christian to live the Mass. His study centers on the ritual acts of the Mass rather than on its origins or on theories.

RYAN, MARY PERKINS. *Perspective for renewal.* Collegeville, Minn.: Liturgical Press, 1960. Pp. v+94p. $2.25.

This small volume is made up of considered judgments on the life of Catholics today as compared to what it ought to be. The view of Christian life as a catalog of do's and don't's does not provide a sense of taking a place in God's redemptive plan. The perspective which Mrs. Ryan offers is a real and truly motivating view of the Christian life.

SHEPPARD, LANCELOT CAPEL. *The liturgical movement.* New York: Hawthorn Books, 1964. Pp. 138. $3.50. (Twentieth century encyclopedia of Catholicism, 115)

This volume of the encyclopedia is an overall survey of the history of the liturgical movement beginning with its monastic origins and coming down to the progress of the present day. Perhaps the second part, which treats fundamental ideas, would have been better placed at the beginning of the book as an introduction.

_____ , ed. *True worship.* Baltimore, Md.: (Helicon) Taplinger, 1963. Pp. xiv+132. $3.50.

Seven papers of a symposium at Downside. The contributors are Father Dalmais, G. Gerbert, L. Bouyer, Father Crichton, Dom Grams, B. Minchin and the editor himself. The papers approach liturgy from a biblical, historical, and pastoral point of view and thus impart a very practical understanding which is at the same time firmly grounded on sound theology.

TAYLOR, MICHAEL J., S.J. *The Protestant liturgical renewal;* a Catholic viewpoint. Westminster, Md.: Newman Press, 1963. Pp. xxi+336. $5.50.

Unfortunately the author omits a treatment of the Episcopalians, but his basic concern is to show how other American Protestants are giving greater emphasis to the Lord's Supper and the sacraments in order to balance their previous emphasis on preaching the Word.

VAGAGGINI, CIPRIANO, O.S.B. *Theological dimensions of the liturgy.* Translated by L. J. Doyle. Collegeville, Minn.: Liturgical Press, 1959. Pp. 300. $3.85.

This is a translation and an abridgment from the second Italian edition of the author's master work, *Il senso teologico della liturgia.* It has little in common with that of one of the other Benedictine writers on the liturgy, Odo Casel. While the latter approaches the subject more intuitively, here we have one of the first attempts to arrive at a firmly based theology of the liturgy.

*VON HILDEBRAND, DIETRICH. *Liturgy and personality.* Rev. ed. Baltimore, Md.: (Helicon) Taplinger, 1960. Pp. 131. $3.50.

The author shows how liturgy tends to develop the human personality, which he says is not a gift but the realization of personal values. The liturgy offers the best means for development because it affords the highest values and orientates them to God, the ultimate value.

IV
ECUMENICS

A. CATHOLIC AUTHORS

*ADAM, KARL. *One and holy.* Translated by C. Hastings. New York: Sheed and Ward, 1951. Pp. 130. $2.00.

An approach to Lutheran-Catholic accord in Germany. The author is completely frank and unapologetic in admitting the corruption in the Church, which precipitated the Reformation. Although written 15 years ago, only in recent times, in the light of II Vatican, have his ideas really come into their own among other thinkers within the Church.

BALTHASAR, HANS URS VON. *Martin Buber and Christianity:* a dialogue between Israel and the Church. Translated by A. Dru. New York: Macmillan, 1961. Pp. 127. $2.50.

This book examines Buber's notions of the faith of Israel. It is the kind of book of which we have too few—deeply thoughtful, highly theological without being tied to a technical vocabulary. The author gives us an insight into the thought of others and presents their viewpoints, even their objections against the Church, with sympathy.

BAUM, GREGORY, O.S.A. *Progress and perspectives:* the Catholic quest for Christian unity. New York: Sheed and Ward, 1962. Pp. 251. $3.95.

The author is a consultant to the Secretariate for Christian Unity in Rome, so his comments are not without authority. He analyzes the meaning of schism in the Church. The book is genuinely irenic and the author has a definite understanding of the inner nature of Protestantism.

_____. *That they may be one.* Westminster, Md.: Newman Press, 1958. Pp. 181. $3.50.

A study of papal doctrine related to the movement for Christian unity from Leo XIII to Pius XII. The approach is theological rather than historical. The author is quite successful in constructing an outline of the theology of Christian unity. Interesting is his view that the function of Catholic ecumenics is not to proselytize, but to stress common Christian elements and to conduct a dialogue on that basis.

BEA, AUGUSTIN CARDINAL, S.J. *The unity of Christians.* Edited by B. Leeming, S.J. New York: Herder and Herder, 1963. Pp. 231. $4.95.

This book is a collection of essays which are at once scholarly and brotherly. The author is the head of the Secretariate for Christian Unity. A notable chapter is the last, "St. Paul's vision of the Church in human history."

BOUYER, LOUIS, C. Or. *The spirit and forms of Protestantism.* Translated by A. V. Littledale. Westminster, Md.: Newman Press, 1956. Pp. 234. $3.75.

Father Bouyer was formerly a Lutheran minister. Here he writes with deep sympathy and shows an understanding of the positive principles of the Reformation. While he admits doctrinal divergencies between Catholics and Protestants, he has made every effort to narrow the abyss between them by passing over non-essential differences.

_____ . *The Word, Church and sacraments in Protestantism and Catholicism.* Translated by A. V. Littledale. New York: Desclee, 1961. Pp. 80. $2.00.

Written in an ecumenical spirit, this is a comparison of three fundamentals: Bible, Church authority, and sacraments.

CARY-ELWES, COLUMBA, O.S.B. *The sheepfold and the shepherd.* London: Longmans, Green, 1961. Pp. 335. $3.00.

Here are outlined the principles of Catholic ecumenism. The author is faithful to his objectives, speaking plainly about the problem of Christian unity and about the more fundamental truths basic to the Catholic position, namely, the nature of the Church and the nature of the papacy.

*CONGAR, YVES, O.P. *Divided Christendom.* London: Geoffry Bles, 1939. Pp. 298. $2.75.

The first technical survey of the ecumenical problem from the viewpoint of Catholic theology. What gives the book particular value is its thorough and profound statement of Catholic doctrine on the Church, her visible and invisible aspects, and their mutual relationship. The whole treatment is based on the notion of the Mystical Body of Christ. Throughout, the author keeps to a *via media,* neither compromising or obscuring principles, nor weakening charity.

DUFF, EDWARD, S.J. *The social thought of the World Council of Churches.* New York: Association Press, 1956. Pp. 339. $7.50.

A study of the origins, structure, philosophy and policy discussions of the W.C.C. Its orientation is toward the social implications of the ecumenical movement, showing the ways in which religious institutions affect and are affected by the social situations of which they are a part.

DUMONT, CHRISTOPHER JEAN, O.P. *Approaches to Christian unity, doctrine and prayer.* Translated by H. St. John. Baltimore, Md.: (Helicon) Taplinger, 1959. Pp. 226. $3.75.

As the subtitle indicates, this book is concerned with the spiritual rather than the administrative or organizational aspects of re-union. This series of 45 meditations provides a prayerful approach to the problem of Catholics and Protestants alike.

HARDON, JOHN A. S.J. *Christianity in conflict:* a Catholic view of Protestantism. Westminster, Md.: Newman Press, 1959. Pp. 300. $4.50.

The subtitle is to be rightly understood as *a* view and not necessarily *the* view. The author, to some extent, lacks a feeling for Protestant theology, though he is sincere in his attempts to dispel some of the widespread ignorance of Protestant thought and opinion among Catholics. Some of the Protestant beliefs which he examines are: the authority of scripture, marriage versus celibacy, questions relating to marital morality, Church and state, religious education, and religious unity movements. He treats these subjects in a clear and interesting manner.

HÄRING, BERNARD, C.SS.R. *The Johannine Council, witness to unity.* Translated by E. G. Kaiser. New York: Herder and Herder, 1963. Pp. 155. $3.50.

The timely and fraternal observations made by this noted theologian are exhilarating and free of polemics. Not a journalistic account of the Council, it focuses on the essentials.

HEENAN, JOHN CARMEL, ed. *Christian unity;* a Catholic view. London: Sheed and Ward, 1962. Pp. 198. $1.50.

In past years great inroads have been made in bringing the ecumenical movement from the level of the theologian down to the level of the parochial clergy and the laity. This book gives prudent direction to encourage the laity to assume a more active role in the work of reuniting Christian Churches. It is realistic in admitting that Catholics are not clamoring for reunion with Protestant denominations, but it is also aware that Catholics are not indifferent. The danger for Catholics, which this book attempts to point out, is that of oversimplification in their approach to ecumenism.

KÜNG, HANS. *The Council, reform and reunion.* Translated by C. Hastings. New York: Sheed and Ward, 1961. Pp. 219. $3.95.

The central and recurring theme of this book is that there can be no reunion of the Church of Rome with her separated brethren until there be a radical reform of Catholicism. In the concluding chapter the author gives some concrete examples where there might be rethinking: papal infallibility, mariology, liturgy, clerical celibacy, the laws of marriage, and the *Index.*

_____. *Structures of the Church.* [See page 48.]

LEEMING, BERNARD, S.J. *The churches and the Church;* a study of ecumenism. Westminster, Md.: Newman Press, 1960. Pp. x+340. $6.50.

In a popular style, this book combines the sure-footedness of an experienced theologian with that sympathy and understanding which are necessary in ecumenical studies. The author's main concern is to build Christian unity. He is concerned with questions pertaining to the relationship between the Catholic Church and the World Council of Churches. This is no deep theological penetration, but a good presentation of the work done by scholars.

McNALLY, ROBERT E., S.J. *Reform of the Church.* New York: Herder and Herder, 1963. Pp. 140. $3.50.

An insight into the Church and reform through an examination of the late Middle Ages. The author shows how the disastrous events of the Medieval Church led to the councils of Vienne, Constance, Basle-Ferrara-Florence, etc. The book is stimulating and provides a good background for a better understanding of the current ecumenical council.

POL, WILLEM HENDRIK VAN DE. *The Christian dilemma.* New York: Philosophical Library, 1953. Pp. 317. $4.75.

The dilemma spoken about is the division between Catholicism and Protestantism. As a convert from Protestantism, the author is in a position to understand both the Protestant and the Catholic points of view. The reader will find this an enlightening study.

SARTORY, THOMAS A. *The oecumenical movement and the unity of the Church.* Translated by H. Graef. Westminster, Md.: Newman Press, 1963. Pp. xx+290. $5.00.

An historical and systematic treatment. The historical part is simply retold, but the systematic part is particularly useful and illuminating. The author portrays a certain versatility as he enters into dialogue not only with German theologians, but also with English, French and Dutch. The book will be more appreciated by professionals than by lay readers.

SAYEGH, MAXIMOS IV, ed. *The Eastern Churches and Catholic unity.* New York: Herder and Herder, 1963. Pp. 237. $4.95.

Western Catholics might be shocked at the forceful and outspoken language found in this book, which is a collection of essays by various Catholic Eastern-rite prelates published in French or Arabic between 1953 and 1962. Their tone reveals profound distress at the division among Christians.

SHERWOOD, POLYCARP, O.S.B., ed. *The unity of the Church of God.* Baltimore, Md.: (Helicon) Taplinger, 1963. Pp. 227. $4.95.

This is a collection of five essays by Catholic and Orthodox scholars on current ecumenical expectations. The two Orthodox representatives point out the necessity of safeguarding Eastern rights; the Catholics concentrate on comparative theology and the historical background for the division of East and West.

SWIDLER, LEONARD, ed. *Dialogue for re-union.* New York: Herder and Herder, 1962. Pp. 88. $1.75. (Quaestiones disputatae, 7)

The four essays which make up this little book were originally lectures in a seminar on ecumenism conducted by the editor at Duquesne University shortly before the opening of Vatican II. The relationship between ecumenism and reform is frequently stressed in all the essays except the first.

TAVARD, GEORGES, A.A. *The Catholic approach to Protestantism.* New York: Harper, 1955. Pp. 160. $2.50.

The author states the need of a positive ecumenical effort among Catholics in this country to respond to the continuing ecumenism among Protestants and to correspond to Catholic efforts already active in Europe. The detailed history of Protestant ecumenism and Catholic reaction to it is enlightening. Of themselves books will not bridge the chasm which has separated Catholicism from Protestantism for more than 400 years, but if enough people were to read books like this one, many would gain the dispositions which will make future reunion possible.

—————. *Holy Writ or Holy Church;* the crisis of the Protestant Reformation. New York: Harper, 1959. Pp. x+250. $5.00.

"Scripture alone" the Reformers are reputed to have said. Catholic theologians have said that revelation has had two sources: scripture and tradition. The author here discusses these two positions and, with a few other contemporary theologians, comes to new conclusions.

—————. *Protestant hopes and Catholic responsibility.* Notre Dame, Ind.: Fides Publishers, 1960. Pp. 63. Pap. $0.75.

A short introduction to the basic principles of Catholic ecumenism. The author says, "The greatest event of our century in the field of religious history is the ecumenical movement. When the political upheavals that we have experienced will be no more than the paragraphs in history books, the ecumenical movement will still be bearing fruit" (p. 9).

—————. *Protestantism.* Translated by D. Attwater. New York: Hawthorn Books, 1959. Pp. 139. $3.50. (Twentieth century encyclopedia of Catholicism, 137)

The author gives evidence of his wide reading in Protestant literature, and he reports fairly. This is a general view of Protestant evolution rather than a series of sketches on various denominations. As such, it is a good, brief survey of Protestantism.

—————. *Two centuries of ecumenism.* Notre Dame, Ind.: Fides Publishers, 1960. Pp. 250. $4.95.

A historical survey of ecumenism in the 19th and 20th centuries. It provides a fairly good history of the movement and is especially useful in bringing to light lesser known personages. The author's message points out the true nature of ecumenism.

TAYLOR, MICHAEL J., S.J. *The Protestant liturgical renewal.* [See page 59.]

*TODD, JOHN. *Catholicism and the ecumenical movement.* London: Longmans, Green, 1956. Pp. 111. $0.90.

This book shows the significance for Catholics, of the World Council of Churches and the movement which it represents. As an introduction to ecumenism it is provocative and will stimulate further study. The author is a layman who has succeeded very well in comprehending the implications of reunion; his treatment is clear and charitable.

WEIGEL, GUSTAVE, S.J. *A Catholic primer on the ecumenical movement.* Westminster, Md.: Newman Press, 1957. Pp. 79. $0.95. (Woodstock papers, 1)

This essay is a compact summary of the ecumenical movement. The first section deals with non-Catholic ecumenism. Another valuable section gives an analysis of ecclesiastical norms which should guide the Catholic in ecumenical work.

_____. *Catholic theology in dialogue.* New York: Harper, 1961. Pp. 126. $2.75.

Lectures given by the author to non-Catholic audiences on theological themes of interest to those in search for Christian unity. In every instance the author endeavors to help Protestants to understand what Catholics believe and why. The author defines ecumenism as the coming together of all Churches professing faith in Jesus Christ, with the hope that some future day they will all be one.

_____. *Churches in North America.* Baltimore, Md.: (Helicon) Taplinger, 1961. Pp. 152. $3.95.

This short volume claims to be an introduction and nothing more. Historical background, geographical origin, and statistics are given for 23 of the more frequently encountered denominations in the U. S.

_____. *Faith and understanding in America.* New York: Macmillan, 1959. Pp. 170. $3.75. Pap. $1.45.

The author is concerned with possibilities and materials available for informal dialogue between Protestants and Catholics in the U. S. His treatment is optimistic and sympathetic.

WILLEBRANDS, J. G. M., and others. *Problems before unity.* Baltimore, Md.: (Helicon) Taplinger, 1962. Pp. 220. $3.50.

Papers given by Catholic theologians from North America and Europe at the 1961 Graymoor Conference. Just how does the Catholic Church view the non-Catholic ecumenical movement? How can we assess the present possibilities for Christian unity? What is the Eastern Orthodox attitude toward the papacy? Can the Catholic layman do anything to bring about the unity of Christians? These are some of the questions confronted.

B. NON-CATHOLIC AUTHORS

*ASMUSSEN, HANS, and others. *The unfinished Reformation.* Translated by R. Olsen. Notre Dame, Ind.: Fides Publishers, 1961. Pp. 213. $4.95.

An attempt by five Lutheran theologians of the *Sammlung* movement to point out what seems to them to be the essential truth of Lutheranism, and to point out how this truth, shorn of accretions, contemporary distortions, and historical misdirections, relates to Roman Catholic teaching. The result is a critique of Lutheranism by Lutherans.

BENOIT, JEAN DANIEL. *Liturgical renewal.* Naperville, Ill.: Allenson, 1958. Pp. 112. Pap. $1.85.

This is a collection of studies on Catholic and Protestant developments in Europe.

BENZ, ERNST. *The Eastern Orthodox Church.* Chicago: Aldine, 1963. Pp. 236. $5.00. Pap. Doubleday (Anchor) $0.95.

A Lutheran expert on the Eastern Churches writes about the thought and life of Orthodoxy. A dispassionate and systematic treatment organized around specific topics. Separate chapters are devoted to dogma, monasticism, the ethical idea of Orthodoxy, etc. The book suggests that mutual trust and understanding have begun to grow between the East and West.

BRILIOTH, YNGVE. *Eucharistic faith and practice;* Evangelical and Catholic. Translated by A. G. Herbert. London: S.P.C.K. Press, 1961. Pp. xvi+295. $3.00.

A timely subject, even though this book was originally published in Sweden in 1930. It is an excellent historical and theological study of the Eucharistic rite as it existed in the early Church, the Middle Ages, the Lutheran tradition, the Anglican tradition, and the Swedish Church.

BROWN, ROBERT McAFEE. *The spirit of Protestantism.* New York: Oxford University Press, 1961. Pp. 284. $5.00.

One of America's leading Protestant theologians writes on the origins, history and meaning of Protestantism. The book contains much that is authentically Christian and is frequently to be applauded, but it is not recommended to one who is not well-grounded theologically, for some of the author's statements warrant a critical evaluation.

CAVERT, SAMUEL McCREA. *On the road to Christian unity.* New York: Harper, 1961. Pp. 192. $3.75.

An appraisal of the ecumenical movement by one of the chief leaders of the World Council of Churches. The book is important for the insight that it provides into the personal feelings, motivations, and thoughts of a devoted ecumenical worker. This subjectivity is also something of a weakness, for the author has equated the W.C.C. with the ecumenical movement, and to a great extent has ignored the efforts of Catholics.

CULLMANN, OSCAR. *Message to Catholics and Protestants.* Translated by J. A. Burgess. Grand Rapids, Mich.: Eerdmans, 1959. Pp. 64. $1.50.

In the process of advocating that an ecumenical offering be taken up once a year in churches of all denominations, this Protestant author says much regarding the union of Protestantism with Catholicism. The tone of the book is one of scientific honesty and sincere concern for the truth.

EDWALL, PEHR. *Ways of worship;* the report of a theological commission of faith and order. New York: Harper, 1951. Pp. 362. $3.50.

This book highlights the fact that the liturgical renewal has had a great influence on the ecumenical consciousness of people of widely differing churches and traditions. It brings together the experiences of several such denominations or confessions. It is a good theological study which portrays the thinking of our separated brethren.

GOODALL, NORMAN. *The ecumenical movement.* 2d ed. New York: Oxford University Press, 1964. Pp. 257. $5.00.

This well-organized history of the ecumenical movement offers the reader both facts and flavor in a flowing, interesting style. It also includes sketches of leading figures in the ecumenical movement. The pages devoted to Catholicism are sympathetic.

LACKMANN, MAX. *The Augsburg Confession and Christian unity.* New York: Herder and Herder, 1963. Pp. xv+159. $4.50.

This work of a Lutheran theologian is a genuine challenge to the Catholic theologian, for Lackmann maintains that the men who drew up the Augsburg Confession of 1530 did not want to cease being Catholics. His work emphasizes what Catholics hold in common with Lutherans and stimulates dialogue on the differences.

LOEWENICH, WALTHER VON. *Modern Catholicism.* Translated by R. H. Fuller. New York: St. Martin's Press, 1959. Pp. viii+378. $9.00.

The author is a Lutheran theologian and a professor of Protestant church history. It is his conviction that modern Catholicism needs to be explained to Protestants. He has tried to be fair and accurate, and this volume will give many Protestants a closer view of Catholicism, even though the author has sometimes misunderstood Catholic teaching.

MACGREGOR, GEDDES. *Corpus Christi;* the nature of the Church according to the Reformed Tradition. London: Macmillan, 1959. Pp. ix+302. $4.20.

An exposition of the nature of the Church according to the Reformed Tradition, in which the idea of the Church is said to find full self-consciousness, and accurate theological definition. The use of emotion is noticeable in the way the image of the Scarlet Woman appears behind every reference to the Catholic Church, and therefore the Catholic reader will see that there are still bridges to be built before we can all be one in Christ.

MACKIE, ROBERT C. and WEST, CHARLES C. *The sufficiency of God;* essays on the ecumenical hope in honor of W. A. Visser 'T Hooft. Philadelphia: Westminster Press, 1963. Pp. 240. $5.50.

Fourteen Protestants and Father Yves Congar have each contributed an essay as a tribute to Visser 'T Hooft, the general secretary of the World Council of Churches. There emerges a biographical sketch of one who has had a real zest for life and for ecumenism.

MCNEILL, JOHN T. *Unitive Protestantism.* The ecumenical spirit and its persistent expression. 2d rev. ed. Richmond, Va.: John Knox Press, 1964. Pp. 352. $4.50.

This is a good general exposition of the Protestant stand on ecumenics. The author traces the unitive principle of Protestantism from the time of the Reformers to the World Council of Churches.

*MASCALL, ERIC LIONEL. *The recovery of unity.* London: Longmans, Green, 1958. Pp. 242. $3.50.

An Anglican theologian describes the bedrock realities of disunity and the starting point for any profitable and constructive thinking about reunion. He insists that Christian union must primarily be a theological concern. The author's erudition makes some demands on his readers. Therefore it is not recommended to one just beginning his investigations into ecumenism.

MEYENDORFF, JEAN. *The Orthodox Church.* Translated by J. Chapin. New York: Pantheon, 1962. Pp. 244. $4.50.

An Orthodox priest-theologian writes on his Church, on its historical development and contemporary relevance. His concluding chapter sets out some hard sayings for the Roman theologian, but their forthright expression will have a therapeutic value for all concerned. It is a useful general introduction to Orthodox Christianity.

*NEILL, STEPHEN CHARLES. *Towards Church union.* Naperville, Ill.: Allenson, 1952. Pp. viii+96. Pap. $1.25.

A survey to approaches to closer union among the churches. This work was published on behalf of the Faith and Order Commission of the World Council of Churches.

NEWBIGIN, J. E. LESSLIE. *The reunion of the Church.* 2d rev. ed. Toronto: Ryerson Press, 1960. Pp. xxxvi+192. $3.75.

The author is now a Presbyterian bishop in India. Essentially his book is an explanation of the theological basis for the infant Church of South India. It is a penetrating study of ecumenism by one who has had first-hand experience.

NIESEL, WILHELM. *Reformed symbolics;* a comparison of Catholicism, Orthodoxy, and Protestantism. Translated by D. Lewis. London: Oliver and Boyd, 1962. Pp. xvi+384. $5.00.

The author, a member of the Reformed Calvinist tradition, examines the theological positions of the main Christian traditions in the light of the one Gospel, as these positions were discovered in Germany during World War II. He clearly makes the points of difference, but at the same time indicates areas for fruitful discussion.

PELIKAN, JAROSLAV. *The riddle of Roman Catholicism.* New York: Abingdon Press, 1959. Pp. 272. $4.00. Pap. $1.50.

A Lutheran theologian interprets Catholicism, its history, beliefs, and future. The riddle which the author tries to unravel is: what happened to the Church since the Reformation, or what makes the Church the way it is today. The book is not a polemic, but an honest search for truth.

RAMSEY, ARTHUR MICHAEL. *An era of Anglican theology:* from Gore to Temple. New York: Scribner's, 1960. Pp. x+192. $2.65.

Stimulating reading, because it contains wide surveys and much information. The 50-years which it covers is a period of Anglican theological ferment.

SCHMEMANN, ALEXANDER. *The historical road to Eastern Orthodoxy.* New York: Holt, Rinehart and Winston, 1963. Pp. 349. $6.50.

A history of Eastern Orthodoxy by a distinguished Orthodox theologian. The presentation is detailed and readable; it unfolds the developments of Orthodoxy from Apostolic times through the early Church councils, the Great Schism, and on down to recent times.

SKYDSGAARD, KRISTEN. *One in Christ.* Translated by A. C. Kildegaard. Philadelphia: Fortress Press, 1957. Pp. iv+220. Pap. $2.25.

An eminent Danish Lutheran theologian explains Protestant and Catholic beliefs, pointing out important similarities and basic differences. This work was originally a series of lectures given at the People's University of Copenhagen and is therefore not a technical expression of theology. It is of significance for Catholics and non-Catholics alike.

—————————., ed. *The papal council and the Gospel.* Minneapolis, Minn.: Augsburg Press, 1961. Pp. 220. $3.95.

Seven Protestant theologians present an anticipatory study of various aspects of II Vatican and their importance for Protestants. They address themselves to Protestants and Catholics alike. The book shows how productive the ecumenical drive has been among Lutherans.

*SOPER, DAVID WESLEY. *Major voices in American theology:* six contemporary leaders. Philadelphia: Westminster Press, 1953. Pp. 217. $3.50.

This is a high-level popularization of pertinent questions in modern theology. It is especially useful in that it presents the positions of those most influential in American Protestantism: Edwin Lewis, Nels Ferré, Paul Tillich, Robert Calhoun and the brothers Reinhold and Richard Niebuhr.

THURIAN, MAX. *The Eucharist memorial.* 2v. Translated by J. G. Davies. V. 1: The Old Testament, V. 2: The New Testament. Richmond, Va.: John Knox Press, 1961. Pap. $1.75 each. (Ecumenical studies in worship, 7 and 8)

The author, one of the founders of the Protestant brotherhood of Taizé, approaches the Eucharist through a biblical theology. He almost presupposes the real presence and our inclusion in Christ's sacrifice and intercession. His views are such that other Protestant theologians have taken him for a Catholic.

_____. *Visible unity and tradition.* Translated by W. J. Kerrigan. Baltimore, Md.: (Helicon) Taplinger, 1962. Pp. 136. $3.50.

Here Thurian writes on the visible unity already existing among Christians and appraises the elements common to the churches, upon which greater unity can be attained. The Catholic reader can subscribe to most of the author's theology; one exception will be his treatment of conciliar authority.

TORRANCE, THOMAS FORSYTH. *Conflict and agreement in the Church.* 2v. V. 1: Order and disorder. V. 2: The ministry and the sacraments of the Gospel. London: Lutterworth Press, 1960. $9.00 and $7.00.

The position of the author as a theologian in the Reformed Tradition has become well known through his editorship of *The Scottish Journal of Theology.* He is definitely not sympathetically inclined toward the Catholic position. Volume one is divided into two parts; the first is his discussions with Anglicans, Presbyterians, and Romans. The second part he devotes to problems of faith and order. In volume two Dr. Torrance deals with questions on the meaning of the ministry and sacraments, questions which ultimately raise the deepest issues between the churches. This is a valuable work in that it shows how a Presbyterian theologian views other Protestants and Catholics.

*VISSER 'T HOOFT, WILHELM, ed. *The first assembly of the World Council of Churches.* Official report. (Amsterdam, 1948) New York: Harper, 1949. Pp. 271. $5.00.

This and the two following works give as full an account of the proceedings of the assemblies as one could expect. The chapters on the sections and committees of the assembly contain full texts of the official reports and summaries of the discussions on them in the plenary sessions.

*_____. *The Evanston Report:* The second assembly of the World Council of Churches. (Evanston, 1954) New York: Harper, 1955. Pp. 368. $5.00.

_____. *The New Delhi Report:* The third assembly of the World Council of Churches. (New Delhi, 1961) New York: Association Press, 1962. Pp. 456. $6.50.

WARE, TIMOTHY. *The Orthodox Church.* Baltimore, Md.: Penguin Books, 1963. Pp. 352. Pap. $1.35.

There has been a long need for a book like this one: an inexpensive and popular study of the Orthodox Church which might satisfy the increasing interest of members of other Christian communities. The author begins tracing the history of the Orthodox Church in Jerusalem and Byzantium, in Russia, Europe and the United States. In the second part of the book he treats of faith and worship, theology, rites and the contribution of the Orthodox to Christian unity.

C. DIALOGUES

*BOSC, JEAN, and others. *The Catholic Protestant dialogue.* Translated by R. J. Olsen. Baltimore, Md.: (Helicon) Taplinger, 1961. Pp. 138. $3.50.

This dialogue is not a debate, but a friendly exchange of ideas between Catholics and Protestants in France. As one would expect in true dialogue, there is an aura of charity; both sides wish to learn from each other, and in turn inform each other. A word of warning is in order for the reader concerning the necessary national adjustments.

BROWN, ROBERT MCAFEE and WEIGEL, GUSTAVE, S.J. *An American dialogue.* Garden City, N.Y.: Doubleday, 1960. Pp. 216. Pap. Anchor (A257) $0.95.

Each author writes a candid account of how the opposite side looks to him in relation to his own faith, and of his own respective place in the world today. Neither author is unaware of the real differences that exist between them; neither stresses merely the similarities. The value of this book is that it is a concrete demonstration of the efficacy of dialogue.

CALLAHAN, DANIEL, ed. *Christianity divided.* New York: Sheed and Ward, 1961. Pp. 335. $6.00.

Essays by well-known Catholic and Protestant theologians on basic theological issues which divide their churches. For serious students of ecumenics or for the late-comer who would like to familiarize himself with ecumenism, this book constitutes a summary of the theological progress of recent years. Some of the papers will be hard to understand without a background in the subject, however.

CHRISTIANS IN CONVERSATION; with a preface by Most Rev. Peter W. Bartholome, bishop of St. Cloud. Westminster, Md.: Newman Press, 1962. Pp. 112. $3.00.

The book contains four papers read at a colloquy of Catholic and Protestant theologians at St. John's Abbey, Collegeville, Minn., in 1960. Jaroslav Pelikan, Raymond T. Bosler, Berthold von Schenk and Godfrey Diekmann discuss issues which divide and factors which unite Catholics and Protestants. Bringing these papers together in one handy volume provides an introduction to the world of ecumenism; or a necessary document for one who has been previously initiated.

MILLER, SAMUEL H. and WRIGHT, G. ERNEST, edd. *Ecumenical dialogue at Harvard:* The Roman Catholic—Protestant colloquium. Cambridge, Mass.: Balknap Press, 1964. Pp. 385. $4.95.

Includes the Charles Chauncey Stillman Lectures by Cardinal Bea. The papers of the other contributors are uniformly excellent, but the dialogue ranges over a broad area touching such subjects as theological reflections on

II Vatican, the interpretation of scripture in biblical studies today, conscience in a pluralistic society and a layman's view of the ecumenical movement.

MORRIS, WILLIAM S., ed. *The unity we seek;* lectures on the Church and the churches. New York: Oxford University Press, 1963. Pp. x +150. Pap. $1.75.

Eight noted Protestant theologians and one Catholic theologian collaborate with the editor in providing the material for this little book, which speaks of the Church as the family of God and points up the necessity of a Catholic —Protestant dialogue. Among the Protestant contributors are Georges Florovsky, George Johnston, Emyln Davies, David Hay and Martin Heinecken. The Catholics are represented by Father Gregory Baum.

PELTON, ROBERT S., ed. *The Church as the body of Christ.* Notre Dame, Ind.: University of Notre Dame Press, 1963. Pp. 145. $2.95. (Cardinal O'Hara series, 1)

This collection results from the second ecumenical colloquium held at Notre Dame. The Protestant participants were K. Skydsgaard and F. Littell; the Catholics were B. Ahern, W. Burghardt, and B. Cooke.

SCHARPER, PHILIP, ed. *American Catholics;* a Protestant—Jewish view. New York: Sheed and Ward, 1959. Pp. 235. $3.75.

In its composition this is an exceptional book. The non-Catholic contributors were asked in charity to assist American Catholics in the never ending self-examination demanded by our commitment to the faith. The book answers the question: "How do American Roman Catholics appear to their Protestant and Jewish neighbors?" Those who contributed to it wrote independently, so that their first contact with the views of fellow contributors came on reading the book itself.

THE WORLD COUNCIL OF CHURCHES: its process of formation. Geneva: World Council Publications, 1946. Pp. 6 +205. $1.50.

This work is comprised of the minutes and reports of a committee meeting held at Geneva from 21 February to 23 February, 1946, and the constitutional documents of the W.C.C. Visser 'T Hooft has written the introduction. It will be a valuable source work for anyone engaged in ecumenism.

V
MORAL THEOLOGY

A. INTRODUCTIONS AND GENERAL WORKS

*ADAM, AUGUST. *The primacy of love.* Translated by C. C. Noonan. Westminster, Md.: Newman Press, 1958. Pp. viii+217. $3.25.

In our society morality has almost become equated with chastity. Dr. Adam analyzes the reasons for this and attempts to establish a genuine Christian hierarchy of virtues, drawing particular attention to the relationship between chastity and charity.

*BOUYER, LOUIS, C.Or. *Christian humanism.* Translated by A. V. Littledale. Westminster, Md.: Newman Press, 1959. Pp. 110. $2.50.

In an age when we are endangered by a stream of pseudo-scientific inference that seems so plausible, a book like this comes as a salutary check-rein. Here the author shows that technology and material progress are not the ultimate objectives of man, but charity.

FORD, JOHN C., S.J. and KELLY, GERALD, S.J. *Contemporary moral theology.* 2v. Westminster, Md.: Newman Press. V. 1: Questions on fundamental moral theology, 1958. Pp. vii+358. $4.50. V. 2: Marriage questions, 1963. Pp. viii+474. $7.50.

The moral problems which engage these authors are not the academic questions discussed by moralists for the past century. Rather, as the title implies, they are problems that have a particular relevance to the contemporary scene. They are handled with competency and balance. The authors show a humanity in judgment that is not always found among moralists.

GILLEMAN, GERARD, S.J. *The primacy of charity in moral theology.* Translated by W. F. Ryan, S.J. and A. Vachon, S.J. Westminster, Md.: Newman Press, 1959. Pp. xxviii+420. $5.50.

The goal of this book is to work out a method of exposition in which charity will play the role of a vital principle in every question of moral theology. The translation is at times a little wooden.

HÄRING, BERNARD, C.SS.R. *The law of Christ:* moral theology for priests and laity. Translated by E. G. Kaiser, C.PP.S. 2v. Westminster, Md.: Newman Press. V. 1: General moral theology, 1961. V. 2: Special moral theology, 1963. $8.50 each.

The author succeeds in bringing together the various branches of theology which have been treated and taught separately. He presents the teachings of the Divine Master as an invitation to follow Christ, to fulfill the moral law out of love rather than from fear of punishment.

HÖRMANN, KARL. *An introduction to moral theology.* Translated by E. Quinn. Westminster, Md.: Newman Press, 1961. Pp. ix+283. $4.95.

The author has succeeded in combining brevity, clarity and accuracy. There is frequent and appealing use made of scripture without abandoning the good features of casuistry.

LECLERCQ, JACQUES. *Christ and the modern conscience.* Translated by R. Matthews. New York: Sheed and Ward, 1962. Pp. 289. $5.00.

This book is a free meditation on a number of concepts in the field of comparative morals. Christian ethics is seen in relation to the ethical traditions of China, India, Greece, Persia, as well as Israel. The similarities are stressed along with the differences. An important distinction made by the author is that between "code morality" and "wisdom morality."

SCHÖLLGEN, WERNER. *Moral problems today.* Translated by E. Quinn. New York: Herder and Herder, 1963. Pp. 236. $4.75.

The author is professor of pastoral medicine at the University of Bonn, and in his native Germany is regarded as second to none in his efforts to enrich moral theology with the fruits of research in anthropology, sociology and physiology. In this book he presents 14 essays which treat of problems in moral and pastoral theology, problems of law and politics, and problems in psychology and medicine. No pat solutions are given for complicated situations, but the author's treatment opens broad avenues for further thought and ultimate solutions.

TILLMANN, FRITZ. *The Master calls;* a handbook of Christian living. Translated by G. J. Roettger, O.S.B. Baltimore, Md.: (Helicon) Taplinger, 1960. Pp. 355. $5.50.

In this new approach to moral theology, the author stresses the fact that Christ rarely mentioned transgressions of the laws of God, but stressed purity of moral activity attained through purity of intention. The general plan of the book reveals this spirit which informs it.

*VON HILDEBRAND, DIETRICH. *Fundamental moral attitudes.* New York: Longmans, Green, 1950. Pp. 72. $1.25.

The book deals with attitudes which make a man moral and which reveal him to others as moral: reverence, faithfulness, awareness of responsibility, veracity, and goodness. These are explained with the serene spiritual overtones characteristic of the author.

B. SPECIAL MORAL PROBLEMS

CALVEZ, JEAN YVES, S.J. and PERRIN, JACQUES. *The Church and social justice.* Chicago: H. Regnery Co., 1961. Pp. xvi+466. $7.50.

Having first appeared in French in 1959, this book has become a standard exposition of the social teaching of the Popes from Leo XIII to Pius XII. "Social" is taken to include all that has to do with those human relationships which grow out of economic matters. Texts and commentary are interwoven to make a coherent whole.

CERVANTES, LUCIUS F., S.J. *And God made man and woman;* a factual discussion of sex differences. Chicago: H. Regnery Co., 1959. Pp. 275. $4.00.

In this book the author, a sociologist and marriage and family counselor, discusses the whole complex, interwoven pattern of masculinity and femininity that enters into human behavior from infancy through adulthood. He presents factual information needed by teachers, parents and married couples.

CRONIN, JOHN FRANCIS, S.S. *Social principles and economic life.* Milwaukee: Bruce, 1959. Pp. 436. $6.50, text edition $5.00.

When published, this book was a major contribution to social thinking in the U. S. The work is well documented, and the author writes with clarity, making his judgments on open issues with fairness and humility.

D'ARCY, ERIC. *Conscience and its right to freedom.* New York: Sheed and Ward, 1961. Pp. x +277. $3.50.

The author is a philosopher-priest. As such he has fairly well succeeded in preparing a sound philosophical argument for the right of conscience to religious freedoms, positive and negative.

FLOOD, PETER, O.S.B., ed. *New Problems in medical ethics.* 4v. Translated by M. G. Carroll. Westminster, Md.: Newman Press, 1953-60. $4.50 each.

These volumes are in the form of a series of papers by French theologians and doctors which were originally presented to a society in Paris, the *Cahiers Laënnec,* in response to a questionnaire sent them by that society. They contain valuable technical information for priests not ordinarily given in moral theology courses, but needed to adequately perform the tasks of confessors and directors of souls.

GARRETT, THOMAS M., S.J. *Ethics in business.* New York: Sheed and Ward, 1963. Pp. 181. $3.95.

The lucid style and tough-minded approach of this work make for interesting reading. The business man will not here find set answers to many vexing problems such as pricing, wages, competition, firing and hiring; rather, he will find a philosophy of business. The book might be described as a stimulating invitation to businessmen and moralists to come together to solve the problems that exist.

GUERRY, EMILE. *The popes and world government.* Translated by G. J. Roettger, O.S.B. Baltimore, Md.: (Helicon) Taplinger, 1964. Pp. xvi +254. $5.50.

The author delineates the teachings of the popes from Leo XIII to John XXIII and Paul VI on world government, which he understands to mean the ideal of a world order of peace and union among peoples based on the natural law as applied to nations and protected by an international governing body. The quotations of papal documents range wide and the analysis is thorough.

HEALY, EDWIN F., S.J. *Medical ethics.* Chicago: Loyola University Press, 1956. Pp. xxii +440. $6.00.

The author tells us that this work was written primarily as a textbook for Catholic medical schools and as a reference book for Catholic hospitals. Priests will often find it useful to consult when they are consulted for advice in practical problems of moral theology.

KELLY, GERALD, S.J. *Medico-moral problems.* St. Louis: Catholic Hospital Association of the United States and Canada, 1958. Pp. 375. $3.00.

This volume comes in answer to the many requests to put a series of five booklets published by the Catholic Hospital Association under one cover. The material has been edited and brought up to date with much new material added. It treats 38 medico-moral problems, with a chapter devoted to each.

LYNCH, WILLIAM F., S.J. *The image industries.* New York: Sheed and Ward, 1959. Pp. 159. $3.50.

Throughout, the author judges the mass media and makes references to the artist, the critic and the theologian. Particularly interesting is his expression of the relationship between art and theology. He suggests a return to the actual.

NEWMAN, JEREMIAH. *Studies in political morality.* Chicago: Scepter Press, 1963. Pp. 459. $6.25.

This is not a book for a politician to use in examining his conscience. Rather, the author's concern is to stake out some of the Church's moral teachings concerning the government of the State. For example, he discusses the origins of political authority, pacificism, Church-state relations, etc.

O'DONNELL, THOMAS JOSEPH, S.J. *Morals in medicine.* 2d ed. revised and enlarged. Westminster, Md.: Newman Press, 1959. Pp. xxi+398. $5.00.

The author is regent of Georgetown University School of Medicine. The index of his book will not be very helpful to the physician who is in a hurry for a practical solution. However, the general contents will be very informative as a useful review of the whole field of medical ethics.

QUILL, JAMES E. *Restitution to the poor;* its origin, nature and extent. Milwaukee: Bruce, 1961. Pp. xiv+141. $3.75.

With the publication of this book, new light was shed on one of the thorniest of moral problems. After a study of the great moralists and canonists, Father Quill shows that the obligation of restitution arises from social justice rather than from commutative justice or positive ecclesiastical law.

ROBERTS, RUFUS P., S.J. *Matrimonial legislation in Latin Oriental canon law;* a comparative study. Westminster, Md.: Newman Press, 1961. Pp. viii+110. $2.95.

This book is concerned with the 707 canons governing the sacrament of matrimony in all the Oriental churches united to Rome. It will not only be useful to the priest who is confronted with mixed-rite marriages, but will make every reader aware of the Church's latest legislation on marriage. It is arranged in parallel columns for the Latin code and the Oriental code, with commentary going across the bottom of the page.

SHEED, FRANK JOSEPH. *The nullity of marriage.* Rev. ed. New York: Sheed and Ward, 1959. Pp. xi+132. $3.00.

This is not a book about marriage, but only about cases where there appears to be marriage but is none. It is directly concerned with Church law and proposes to show that the Church's law on nullity is a strong and clearly defined system, carefully reasoned and consistent with itself.

THOMAS, JOHN L., S.J. *Marriage and rhythm.* Westminster, Md.: Newman Press, 1957. Pp. ix+180. $3.00.

Here the moralist will find a brief, intelligent summary of various social forces affecting the American Catholic family, and of the particular relevance to the moral judgement of the liceity of rhythm as a means of limiting conception. It can also be illuminating for a couple contemplating marriage.

VANN, GERALD, O.P. *Morals and man.* Rev. ed. New York: Sheed and Ward, 1960. Pp. 223. $3.50.

Although this book is not the fruit of original research, it is scholarly in its positive approach and in its freedom from casuistry. There are lengthy quotes from other authors, but when Vann himself speaks the style is rich and free from the technical language of a textbook. The subjects treated include: the problem of freedom, the search for happiness, Thomist moral theology, Thomism and integration, politics and personalism, Christian marriage, diversity in worship, divine transcendence and sorrow.

*VON HILDEBRAND, DIETRICH. *In defense of purity*. Rev. ed. Baltimore, Md.: (Helicon) Taplinger, 1962. Pp. 142. $3.50.

Here are insights into purity both for the married and unmarried which cannot but move the heart and fill the soul with a new light. This is a great book, first published in 1931 and for some time out of print, now in a revised edition for a new generation.

VI
CHURCH HISTORY

A. INTRODUCTIONS AND GENERAL WORKS

BARRY, COLMAN J., O.S.B. *Readings in church history.* 2v. Westminster, Md.: Newman Press, 1960 and 1965. $7.50 each. Pap. $2.95 each.

This is a compilation of source materials from a wide range of social, economic, political, intellectual, theological, and mystical writings, many of which have hitherto been untranslated or not easily accessible. Volume one covers the period from Pentecost to the Protestant Revolt, volume two from the Reformation to the French Revolution. The selections are arranged chronologically and preceded by informative introductions by the editor.

DANIÉLOU, JEAN, S.J. *The Lord of history.* Chicago: H. Regnery Co., 1958. Pp. viii+375. $6.00.

The title adequately indicates the subject of this book and the author's thesis. He states that history is unintelligible without a Christo-centric basis and that salvation is the distinguishing feature of sacred, as opposed to secular, history.

D'ARCY, MARTIN, S.J. *The meaning and matter of history;* a Christian view. New York: Farrar Straus, 1959. Pp. 309. $5.50. Pap. Meridian (M110) $1.75.

The author presents a penetrating argument for the claim that Christianity can shed light on the record of human experience. His book traces the growth of the philosophy of history from Thucydides to Toynbee.

DAWSON, CHRISTOPHER H. *Religion and the rise of Western culture.* New York: Sheed and Ward, 1950. Pp. xvi+286. $3.50. Pap. Image (D64) $0.85.

Those who have to grapple with problems arising from the cultural gulf between the ages of faith and the present day will find much to aid them in this work. In his introductory chapter the author speaks of the significance of the Western development. From the beginnings of the Church and the time of the barbarians he traces history down to the thirteenth century. The presentation is solid, and at the same time clear, well-knit, and civilized.

HUGHES, PHILIP. *Popular history of the Catholic Church.* New York: Macmillan, 1947. Pp. xii+294. $6.50. Pap. $1.95.

In a work that is well planned and balanced, the learned historian, Father Hughes, gives us a succinct presentation of Church history down to the pontificate of Pius XII. The style is lively, enriched with vivid phrases and a refreshing candor.

MIRGELER, ALBERT. *Mutations of Western Christianity.* Translated by E. Quinn. New York: Herder and Herder, 1964. Pp. x+158. $4.50.

The author does not here present a history of the Church. Assuming his readers to have some background in European history, he evaluates some of the turning points in history such as the conversion of Constantine, the evangelization of the Germans, the coronation of Charlemagne, and the entrance of the papacy into world politics in its contest with the Empire. His views are often original, arresting, and even provocative.

WALKER, WILLISTON. *A history of the Christian Church.* Rev. ed. New York: Scribner's, 1959. Pp. 585. $7.25.

The revision of this Protestant classic was effected by several professors of Union Theological Seminary, New York. Sections were added, and there was a more radical reworking of some material, particularly in the modern period, in order to bring the text up to date. The original was written in 1918 and has been a favorite ever since.

B. THE EARLY CHURCH

ALTANER, BERTHOLD. *Patrology;* writings and teachings of the Church Fathers. Translated by H. Graef. New York: Herder and Herder, 1958. Pp. 659. $10.00.

From Abercius to Zozimus, everyone who was of any significance among the Fathers is included in this valuable work on the early Church. It is the only one-volume work on patristic studies available in the English language.

*CHADWICK, OWEN. *John Cassian.* New York: Cambridge University Press, 1950. Pp. xi+213. $3.00.

A monograph on the earliest western monastic theorist. It can be characterized as a critical synthesis and at the same time a judicious interpretation of its subject. The style is a bit ponderous but the work is sincere, frank, and honest.

CONGAR, YVES, O.P. *After nine-hundred years;* the background of the schism between the Eastern and Western Churches. New York: Fordham University Press, 1959. Pp. ix+150. $4.50.

The traditional date for the Eastern Schism is 1054, but the author shows that the seeds for the break between the East and the West were sown many centuries before. He concludes that only in the atmosphere of the love and forgiveness suggested by Pope John XXIII can these wounds be healed.

CROSS, FRANK LESLIE. *The early Christian Fathers.* Naperville, Ill.: Allenson, 1960. Pp. 218. $3.50.

Good for one preparing to "walk with the Fathers" in original texts as well as in translations. The style is crisp, clear, concise, and anything but pedantic. This volume, the first of a projected three, goes up to the early fourth century.

DANIEL-ROPS, HENRY. *The Church of Apostles and martyrs.* Translated by A. Butler. New York: Dutton, 1960. Pp. 623. $10.00. Pap. 2v. Image (D128A and B) $1.35 each.

As the title implies, the book begins with a study of the infant Church. It includes chapters on St. Paul, the persecutions and the catacombs, the liturgy, and early Christian literature. It closes with the time of Theodosius, who established Christianity as the official State religion on the eve of the barbarian invasions. The book is not for scholars, but it is written by a scholar.

GRANT, ROBERT M. *Gnosticism and early Christianity.* New York: Columbia University Press, 1959. Pp. 227. $4.50.

The author's thesis is that gnosticism arose out of the debris of apocalyptic-eschatological hopes which were shattered in the fall of Jerusalem. A good study of a heretical trend that has long influenced the Church.

*GREENSLADE, STANLEY LAWRENCE. *Schism in the early Church.* New York: Harper, 1953. Pp. 247. $3.75.

The publication of this book grew out of the Edward Cadbury Lectures given by the author in the years 1949-50. In it he examines what happened in the first five centuries of the Church. After he points up some of the problems in the early Church he makes his practical application for the interests of the Church today.

*MARROU, HENRI. *St. Augustine and his influence through the ages.* London: Longmans, 1957. Pp. 192. $1.35.

About half the book is taken up with a selection of Augustine's writings, the rest consists of an account of Augustine's life, works and personality, and a summary but interesting account of his influence down to the present day. Mr. Marrou points out that the particular value of Augustine's teaching is that he instructs us by his example in the art of living through an age of catastrophe.

QUASTEN, JOHANNES. *Patrology.* 3v. Westminster, Md.: Newman Press, 1950-1960. $6.00, $6.75, $7.00.

Father Quasten, author and eminent scholar, was dean of the faculty of sacred theology at The Catholic University of America from 1945-49. The contents and tone of these volumes are faithful to his objective, viz., to initiate the student into the knowledge and love of the Fathers. Besides being an introductory tool for the student, it serves as an excellent reference work for scholars.

SELLERS, ROBERT VICTOR. *The Council of Chalcedon:* a historical and doctrinal survey. Naperville, Ill.: Allenson, 1953. Pp. xviii+361. $6.50.

The period treated in this book is one of the most intricate periods in the history of dogma. The book recounts in detail the long and involved history of the politico-theological issues at stake in the great Christological disputes of which the Council of Chalcedon was the focal point. Although the facts are presented, frequently they are not interpreted for the reader.

WOLFSON, HARRY AUSTRYN. *The philosophy of the Church Fathers:* Faith, Trinity, Incarnation. Cambridge, Mass.: Harvard University Press, 1956. Pp. xxviii+635. $10.00.

Here the author studies the use which the Church Fathers made of Greek philosophy to express the dogmas indicated in the subtitle. Rather than a history of philosophy, this is more a history of the theological process. In any case, the author writes as an historian, not as a theologian.

C. THE MEDIEVAL CHURCH

BENZ, ERNST. *The Eastern Orthodox Church;* its thought and life. Translated by Richard and Clara Winston. Chicago: Aldine, 1963. Pp. vi+230. $5.00. Pap. Anchor $0.95.

Ernst Benz is a contemporary German Protestant theologian. One of the best features of his work is that he shows the difference between Eastern and Western thinking. He rightly emphasizes the well-nigh inseparability of dogma and ritual, belief and action in the Orthodox mind. Such considerations as are presented here will go far in clearing up the confusion that has arisen from too close a comparison between Catholic and Orthodox Christians.

COULTON, GEORGE GORDON. *Medieval village, manor and monastery.* New York: Peter Smith, 1960. Pp. 603. $4.50. Pap. Harper Torchbks. (Tb1022) $2.75.

While this is not a thorough synthesis, but rather a series of tableaus, and while it is true that the author writes with a strong anti-Catholic bias, it will be useful to priests and students of Catholic theology, who have for perhaps too long thought of the 13th century solely as the greatest of centuries. The author has pointed out some dark spots of that time.

DANIEL-ROPS, HENRY. *The Church in the Dark Ages.* New York: Dutton, 1959. Pp. 624. $10.00. Pap. 2v. Image $1.35 each.

This is a notable contribution to ecclesiastical history, covering the period from St. Augustine to the year 1000. The author shows good control of documentary evidence, a wide knowledge of modern scholarship and judicious impartiality.

DAWSON, CHRISTOPHER H. *The making of Europe.* New York: Sheed and Ward, 1946. Pp. xxiv+317. $4.50.

Instead of treating the Dark Ages as a formless waste of barbarianism and decay, the author views it as the formative period of European history, the first element of European unity. The second element is the Catholic Church, and the third, the classical tradition. These are the three pillars on which Europe was built.

DEANESLY, MARGARET. *A history of the Medieval Church.* 10th ed. London: Methuen, 1959. Pp. viii+284. $4.95.

This short study was planned for the use of both the general reader and for students of theology. It gives some idea of the medieval attitude towards life, religion, and the church, of the faith and ideals of medieval churchmen, and of the actual working of the medieval church system. The author considers the middle ages to begin with the pontificate of Gregory the Great and to end before the Reformation.

DUCKETT, ELEANOR SHIPLEY. *Carolingian portraits;* a study in the ninth century. Ann Arbor: University of Michigan Press, 1962. Pp. 311. $5.95.

Dealing with the period under Charlemagne and his successors, the author allows these personages to speak for themselves through translations of noteworthy passages from their writings. The specialist will confer Migne, but here is a select collection for the amateur historian.

——————. *The gateway to the Middle Ages.* Ann Arbor: University of Michigan Press, 1938. In 3 parts: 1. Italy, Pp. 153. 2. France and Britain, Pp. 219. 3. Monasticism, Pp. 262. $4.40 each. Pap. Ann Arbor Books (AA 449 — AA451) $1.75 each.

This is a work which gives evidence of the author's scholarship and her gift for narration. It is an instructive and delightful survey of the 6th century, treating all the great men of the day.

GILSON, ETIENNE. *History of Christian philosophy in the Middle Ages.* New York: Random House, 1955. Pp. 829. $8.75.

The verdict of the author is that during the Middle Ages the Gospel changed philosophy from the natural pagan science of the Greeks into an intrinsically Christian science, because this philosophy was structured within the framework of Christian theology. This work, on the plan of a textbook, is indispensable to anyone with a serious interest in scholasticism.

——————. *Reason and revelation in the Middle Ages.* Translated by L. R. Ward. New York: Scribner, 1938. Pp. 114. $2.50. Pap. $1.25.

The renowned medievalist and philosopher has been criticized by some of his colleagues for his manner of relating faith and reason. Perhaps this is the book which precipitated such criticism. In three parts he treats the primacy of faith, the primacy of reason, and the harmony between reason and revelation.

GIMPEL, JEAN. *The cathedral builders.* Translated by C. Barnes Jr. New York: Peter Smith, 1960. Pp. 192. $3.25. Pap. Grove (Evergreen P21) $1.35.

From the 11th to the 13th century, the period covered by the author in this study, there was more stone quarried in France alone than in the entire history of ancient Egypt. Hence this book focuses on one of the greatest outbursts of creative genius in the history of man. Its lucid style and the copious illustrations provide interesting and informative reading.

HEER, FRIEDRICH. *The medieval world:* Europe 1000-1350. Translated by J. Sondheimer. Cleveland: World Publishing Co., 1962. Pp. 365. $7.00. Pap. Mentor (MQ524) $0.95.

A series of 16 essays developing the thesis that from the 12th to the 15th centuries the intellectual, social, political and spiritual climate of Europe underwent a radical change. As a rule, the author skillfully presents data to substantiate his judgments.

KNOWLES, DAVID. *The evolution of medieval thought.* Baltimore, Md.: (Helicon) Taplinger, 1962. Pp. 356. $5.95. Pap. Vintage (V246) $1.95.

Difficult ideas are clearly expressed as the author surveys the history of medieval thought, from its antecedents in Plato, Aristotle and Plotinus down to its decline in the 14th century. Very profitable reading to obtain a feeling for the medieval period.

LECLERCQ, JEAN, O.S.B. *The love of learning and the desire for God.* New York: Fordham University Press, 1960. Pp. 415. $5.50.

One of the most eminent medievalists of our day shows how the monk achieved the reconciliation of the study of letters and an unimpeded search for God. His work highlights the apostolic nature of scholarship and the fact that this apostolate was the motivation of Catholic learning all through the centuries.

OBERMAN, HEIKO A. *The harvest of medieval theology.* Cambridge, Mass.: Harvard University Press, 1963. Pp. xv+495. $9.25.

This is a thorough discussion of the feud which raged between nominalism and realism. While the author leans toward the glorification of nominalism, one cannot say that he is historically unobjective in his observations.

SOUTHERN, RICHARD WILLIAM. *The making of the Middle Ages.* New York: Yale University Press, 1953. Pp. 280. $4.50. Pap. $1.95.

The author begins his treatise on the Middle Ages only after they had already attained a certain character, i.e. in 972. His work on the 11th and 12th centuries is especially impressive. Due to his personal approach to the presentation of material, the reader may sense a lack of coherence, for the contents of the book seem to be a series of tableaus placed in juxtaposition. But for all of this, what the author has to say is most illuminating and comes from the pen of a first-rate scholar. David Knowles has said that Mr. Southern's knowledge in the sphere of religious and monastic history is probably unsurpassed by any other English writer.

D. THE REFORMATION

BAINTON, ROLAND HERBERT. *Here I stand!* New York: Abingdon Press, 1959. Pp. 429. $5.50. Pap. Apex Books, $1.75, Mentor (MT310) $0.75.

The author is neither a German nor is he Lutheran, and therefore he is free from a patriotic bias in presenting a candid biography of Martin Luther. It is well-based, popularly written, and truly an exciting book.

—————. *The Reformation of the sixteenth century.* New York: Peter Smith, 1956. Pp. 276. $3.75. Pap. Beacon, $1.60.

One cannot recommend this book as heartily as one would like, because the author makes some erroneous statements which might go unnoticed by the unwary. Yet it is an excellent outline of the period and can serve as a good supplement to a more objective coverage of the same material.

DANIEL-ROPS, HENRY. *The Catholic Reformation.* Translated by J. Warrington. New York: Dutton, 1962. Pp. 435. $10.00.

The title is somewhat misleading, because it treats not a period of time but a stage of development in the Church, and then not on a universal basis but only in the Church of France. Although the information contained in this work comes from secondary sources, it is interestingly presented.

—————. *The Protestant Reformation.* Translated by A. Butler. New York: Dutton, 1961. Pp. 560. $10.00. Pap. 2v. Doubleday (Image) $1.35 each.

This is the fourth volume of the author's 10-volume history of the Church of Christ. It is a popular synthesis blessed with literary grace as well as with the scholarliness which usually characterizes the author. Its personal approach makes its reading both a pleasure and an education.

GEYL, PIETER. *The revolt of the Netherlands.* 2d ed. New York: Barnes and Noble, 1958. Pp. 310. $6.00.

This is a standard work, a reinterpretation of the revolt against Spanish domination. It compresses an enormous amount of detail into a comparatively small space and attempts to remain free of historic prejudices. Since it is a synthesis of existing studies, it will better serve the layman than the professional who is interested in primary sources.

GRIMM, HAROLD J. *The Reformation era, 1500-1650.* New York: Macmillan, 1954. Pp. 675. $6.95.

Herein the author has attempted to tell the story of the rise of Protestantism and the Catholic reforms in their complete setting. This one-volume work is a good, objective overview of all religious movements up to the middle of the 17th century. It is well written and eminently readable.

HALLER, WILLIAM. *The rise of Puritanism.* New York: Harper and Row, 1957. Pp. 464. Pap. Torchbks. (Tb22) $2.25.

This study was undertaken by the author in an attempt to understand Milton and his relation to Puritanism. The study closes with the year 1643. It is one of the most satisfactory and scholarly studies of the whole Puritan movement.

HUGHES, PHILIP. *Popular history of the Reformation.* Garden City, N.Y.: Doubleday, 1957. Pp. 343. $4.00. Pap. Image (D92) $0.95.

What makes this study particularly interesting even to one who thinks he knows his Reformation history, is its richness in concrete detail. It will remain a long time a standard popular treatment of the Reformation.

LEYS, MARY DOROTHY ROSE. *Catholics in England, 1559-1829;* a social history. New York: Sheed and Ward, 1962. Pp. 220. $4.00.

With brevity and yet with a fine sense for historical detail, the author presents a work which was not intended for specialists or for those interested in controversy. She merely tries to examine the relations that existed between Catholics and their neighbors at a time when the practice of the faith was banned by law.

LORTZ, JOSEPH. *How the Reformation came.* New York: Herder and Herder, 1964. Pp. 115. $2.95.

This is an English popularization of *Die Reformation in Deutschland,* the classic work by Father Lortz who is a noted German historian. He portrays Luther as the personification of old, overdue demands which were universally justified. In these terms he re-echoes the sentiments of John XXIII, that the greatest obstacle to the spread of the Gospel in our day is divided Christianity. The reader is repeatedly impressed by the author's historical objectivity, Christian charity, and ecumenical spirit.

POWICKE, FREDERICK M. *The Reformation in England.* New York: Oxford University Press, 1941. Pp. vi+137. Pap. $1.25.

This is not a history of the religious revolt in England, but an attempt to explain how the transition from the medieval system to the Church of Tudor times was effected, and the changes which this transition involved. The author brings into bold relief the fact that the people were quite confused about the whole matter.

*TIERNEY, BRIAN. *The foundations of the conciliar theory.* New York: Cambridge University Press, 1955. Pp. 280. $5.00.

Although written some ten years ago, this is still a timely study. The author, an American medievalist, shows how the tenets of the conciliarists were a logical culmination of the collegial theory of canon law, rather than an outgrowth of the governmental practices of temporal monarchs.

WHITNEY, JAMES POUNDER. *History of the Reformation.* 2d ed. Naperville, Ill.: Allenson, 1940. Pp. xv+526. $5.00.

More complete on Trent than many other books, this work is specially marked by calmness, detachment, and an irenical spirit. For a lack of completeness it could not be said to be a definitive work, yet there is much of value included in these pages by a noted Reformation historian.

E. THE POST-REFORMATION

BROWN, ROBERT McAFEE. *The spirit of Protestantism.* New York: Oxford University Press, 1961. Pp. 248. $5.00, text edition $3.00.

This is a Protestant seminary professor writing about Protestantism. For those with the necessary background it will be profitable reading, because it provides an accurate picture of the way many American Protestants today conceive of the Christian message.

CHADWICK, OWEN, ed. *The mind of the Oxford Movement.* Stanford, Calif.: Stanford University Press, 1960. Pp. 239. $4.25.

Where this study excels is in the author's historical perspective. He traces the whole High Church tradition and shows why the tradition needed new principles to back it in 1830. Further, the author hints at the fact that what was basic to the crisis was the Church's authority in relation to the State.

CONNOLLY, JAMES M. *The voices of France.* New York: Macmillan, 1961. Pp. 231. $5.95.

This book presents much detail and background on names and trends. It is a broad study of the recent flowering of theological thought in France, and attempts to evaluate its intellectual significance. The author presupposes some background for his knowledgeable presentation.

DANSETTE, ADRIEN. *Religious history of modern France.* 2v. Translated by J. Dingle. New York: Herder and Herder, 1961. $16.50 set.

The cordial reception which this work enjoyed after its translation from French proved the need for a re-evaluation and a new approach to Church-State relations in France since 1789. The specialist author has presented a readable work, for the reader has been spared the drudgery of wading through footnotes.

DRUMMOND, ANDREW L. *German Protestantism since Luther.* Naperville, Ill.: Allenson, 1951. Pp. x+282. $6.50.

The author has attempted to sketch the general evolution of German Protestantism and to fill in the outline with enough detail to give substance and vitality to the skeleton. He begins his account with the death of Luther in 1546 and comes down to 1948. Part I is entitled: Church and Religion; Part II, Church and State.

HALES, EDWARD ELTON YOUNG. *Revolution and the Papacy, 1769-1846.* Garden City, N.Y.: Hanover House, 1960. Pp. 320. $4.20. Pap. $0.95.

A survey of the history of the Holy See from Clement XIV to Gregory XVI, largely in terms of the relationship between the temporal power of the popes and the main political doctrines of the time. A timely book, now that the relationship between Church and world politics is again being discussed.

HAZARD, PAUL. *European thought in the eighteenth century.* Translated by J. L. May. New York: Peter Smith, 1954. Pp. 477. $4.75.

Covering the period from Montesquieu to Lessing, this book describes the national characteristics of the age of romanticism. It is an illuminating interpretation of a vital period in European thought.

HUGHES, PHILIP. *Rome and the Counter-Reformation in England.* London: Burnes, Oates, 1942. Pp. ix+446. $3.50.

The first two parts of this book are a digest of the work that has been done on the Counter-Reformation Movement. Although the material is not new, the author is to be praised for his many interesting observations and his arresting approach. In the third and final part of the book Father Hughes gives us the results of his own special studies on Dr. Richard Smith, Bishop of Chalcedon.

JANELLE, PIERRE. *The Catholic Reformation.* Milwaukee: Bruce, 1949. Pp. xiv+397. Pap. $2.25.

Obviously it is impossible to deal with every phase and circumstance of so vast a movement as the Catholic Counter-Reformation. The prime value of this work is that the author has made available an adequate and readable record of its most salient features. The treatment is candid as well as thorough.

KINGDON, ROBERT McCUNE. *Geneva and the coming of the wars of religion in France, 1555-1563.* New York: Gregory Lounz, 1956. Pp. ix+163. $6.00.

A valuable monograph and a solid contribution to Reformation history. The author did extensive research in the archives of Geneva. Whenever he ventures an opinion beyond the confines of his sources he does not fail to indicate the lack of positive evidence.

KNOX, RONALD A. *Enthusiasm.* New York: University of Oxford Press, 1950. Pp. viii+622. $6.00.

The author has called this work the whole of his literary life, the unique child of his thought. It took him 30 years to write it. It is "a chapter in the history of religion, with special reference to the 17th and 18th centuries." As such it runs the gamut of heresies from Marcionism, Montanism and Donatism, down to Jansenism, Quietism and Methodism. This book remains alone in the field without any rival. It will appeal not only to the scholar, but to every educated man interested in the spiritual history of the past.

MCNEILL, JOHN T. *The history and character of Calvinism.* New York: Oxford University Press, 1954. Pp. 466. $5.50.

Most important for showing the Zwinglian background, and for giving biographical and historical discussions of Calvin in Geneva and Strassbourg. In general it is a scholarly yet readable discussion based on primary sources.

WAND, JOHN WILLIAM CHARLES. *A history of the modern Church from 1500 to the present day.* 7th rev. ed. New York: London House, 1952. Pp. 314. $4.95.

The author is the editor of the *Church Quarterly Review.* This book was first published in 1930 and is perhaps still one of the best single volume surveys.

F. HISTORY OF THE CHURCH IN AMERICA

BARRY, COLMAN, J., O.S.B. *The Catholic Church and German Americans.* Washington, D.C.: Catholic University of America Press, 1953. Pp. 348. $5.75.

This account of the great contribution made by German Catholics to the Church in this country and to the nation itself is based on source materials gathered from archives on both sides of the Atlantic. The literary style and fascinating descriptions make this work enjoyable reading.

CATHOLICISM IN AMERICA. New York: Harcourt, Brace, 1954. Pp. viii+242. $3.75.

A collection of literature which has grown up as an apologetic against each successive wave of anti-Catholicism in America, would present a fairly good picture of the growth of the Church in America. Here we have a collection of essays which appeared in *Commonweal* during 1953 which deal with one such period, the post-World War II manifestation of anti-Catholicism in American life known as Blanshardism.

EBERHARDT, NEWMAN C., C.M. *A survey of American church history.* St. Louis: B. Herder Book Co., 1964. Pp. ix+308. Pap. $2.95.

The author's aim is to provide students and general readers with a brief, yet not utterly superficial outline of American church history. This book can help lead readers deeper into the subject. Also helpful is the 20-page bibliography which the author has appended to his work.

ELLIS, JOHN TRACY. *American Catholicism.* Chicago: University of Chicago Press, 1956. Pp. xiii+207. $3.00. Pap. $1.75.

A definitive history of the Church in this country has not yet been written. The merit of this work is that it provides the student of secular American history with a parallel study of religious history, which often played a great role in the formation of our nation.

―――――. *Documents of American Catholic history.* Rev. ed. Milwaukee: Bruce, 1956. Pp. xxii+667. $8.50.

A collection of documents such as these answers a long-felt need. It will help the average student of American Church history get to the original sources pertinent to the field. The book has special merit in making available those documents which cannot easily be found anywhere else.

*GUILDAY, PETER. *A history of the councils of Baltimore 1791-1884.* New York: Macmillan, 1932. Pp. x+291. $3.00.

This is still the best general work on national and provincial conciliar legislation of the Catholic Church in the United States.

―――――. *An introduction to church history.* St. Louis: B. Herder Book Co., 1925. Pp. vii+350. $2.00.

First after John Gilmary Shea, Msgr. Guilday was a pioneer in the systematic, critical study of the Church in the U.S. This excellent book contains the author's seminary principles for research methods in Church history developed during the time when he was a professor at the Catholic University of America.

HANLEY, THOMAS O'BRIEN. *Their rights and liberties.* Westminster, Md.: Newman Press, 1959. Pp. xv+142. $2.75.

It is the burden of Father Hanley's book to trace the traditions which inspired the beginnings of religious and political freedom in Maryland. Footnotes are relegated to the end for an easier reading of the text proper.

McAVOY, THOMAS T., C.S.C. *The Americanist heresy in Roman Catholicism.* Notre Dame, Ind.: University of Notre Dame Press, 1963. Pp. 322. Pap. $1.95.

The heresy of Americanism which was condemned by Leo XIII proved to be more hypothetical than real, but its effects were felt for a long time among the American hierarchy. This book fills a lacuna in American Church history.

―――――, ed. *Roman Catholicism and the American way of life.* Notre Dame, Ind.: University of Notre Dame Press, 1960. Pp. viii+248. $4.50.

This work consists of eighteen essays by various contributors. The first part treats of Roman Catholicism in the 20th century in America; and the second part takes up the immigration question and how it affected American Catholicism.

MAYNARD, THEODORE. *The story of American Catholicism.* 2v. Garden City, N. Y.: Doubleday (Image 106a and b) Pap. $0.95.

The author is not an historian. Neither is the work which he produced a history. As its title implies it is a story—most interesting opinions of the author on American Catholic developments. As a popularization, it makes very interesting reading.

MURRAY, JOHN COURTNEY, S.J. *We hold these truths.* New York: Sheed and Ward, 1961. Pp. 336. $5.00.

The 13 chapters of this book are based on occasional papers and addresses delivered by the author over a period of about ten years. In discussing some of the pressing problems of American Catholicism such as federal aid to education, freedom of religion and toleration, the tradition of reason in politics, he refuses to depart from objective principle. His treatment of the natural law will continue to annoy non-Catholic readers.

ONG, WALTER, S.J. *Frontiers in American Catholicism.* New York: Macmillan, 1957. Pp. 125. $2.50. Pap. $1.25.

A very optimistic view of the theological meaning of our age, and more particularly of American Catholicism. With keen perception the author points out new challenges to the Church of America—challenges that are comparable to those of the frontier, the spirit of enterprise, exploration, and expansion.

SWEET, WILLIAM WARREN. *The story of religion in America.* Rev. ed. New York: Harper and Row, 1950. Pp. xiv+338. $3.75.

Since its first edition in 1930, this book has done much to influence the minds of American church historians and to stimulate further interest in the subject. It is a good comprehensive survey of the elements which go to form the religious picture of our country.

WEIGEL, GUSTAVE, S.J. *Faith and understanding in America.* New York: Macmillan, 1959. Pp. 170. $3.75. Pap. $1.45.

While Father Weigel will always be remembered as a renowned ecumenist, here he has little to say on ecumenism as such. Rather he is concerned with the possibilities for a dialogue between Catholics and Protestants in the U. S. on an informal level.

G. SPECIAL TOPICS

BAINTON, ROLAND HUBERT. *The travail of religious liberty.* Philadelphia: Westminster Press, 1951. Pp. 272. $4.00.

The subject is one that has been cast into sharp relief again by Vatican II. By means of nine biographies the author discusses freedom of conscience. Most of these studies were originally delivered by the author while a guest lecturer at Union Theological Seminary, Richmond, Va.

BILLINGTON, RAY ALLEN. *The Protestant crusade; 1800-1860.* New York: Peter Smith, 1952. Pp. viii+514. $6.50.

In the years since 1938, when this book was first published, it has stood the test of time. No one has found any serious defects in it. It is a thoroughly documented study of the origins of American nativism, presented in an unbiased, scholarly way.

JEDIN, HUBERT. *Ecumenical councils of the Catholic Church.* Translated by E. Graf. New York: Herder and Herder, 1960. Pp. 253. $3.95. Pap. Paulist Press, $0.95.

From Nicea to Vatican I, the great councils of the Church which defined the teachings of Christ are here discussed by a Roman Catholic. The author writes like a skilled journalist, emphasizing human interest features and factual reporting without bias or polemics.

JOHN, ERIC, ed. *The popes:* a concise biographical history. New York: Hawthorn Books, 1964. Pp. 496. $15.00.

This is a series of biographical articles for each of the popes. Every entry is a model of historical precision, concise, accurate, and careful to distinguish legend from fact. The presentation is factual and objective. The men who collaborated in its production are all distinguished British scholars.

*KNOWLES, DAVID. *The English mystical tradition.* New York: Harper and Row, 1961. Pp. viii+197. $3.75.

This book is a masterpiece of verbal economy. The author handles theological themes with almost the same facility with which he has for long handled the most intricate historical controversies. As he discusses the English mystics he brings his reader up to date regarding the interpretations of modern historians.

MOORMAN, JOHN RICHARD HUMPIDGE. *A history of the Church of England.* New York: Morehouse-Barlow Co., 1954. Pp. xx+460. $7.50.

The author does a masterful job in compressing the history of 1750 years into 400 pages, and comes up with a good introduction and guide to the history of the Church of England. In drawing up his account he begins with the first preaching of the Word in England and comes down to the present day. The author presents this account as a story, and he does not claim to be free of bias. There are 4 parts: The Roman and Anglo-Saxon period, The Middle Ages, The Reformation and after, and The Industrial Age.

*ROUSE, RUTH and NEILL, STEPHEN CHARLES, edd. *A history of the ecumenical movement, 1517-1948.* Philadelphia: Westminster Press, 1954. Pp. 822. $9.00.

A standard account, in 16 chapters. The first three deal with the 16th, 17th, and 18th centuries. Chapter 5 and following give developments for unity in 19th century America and Europe. In chapter 15 the Roman Catholic attitude toward the development of the World Council of Churches is outlined fairly and concisely. The greater portion of the book is devoted to the 20th century, particularly the activities of the Conferences on Faith, Law and Order, beginning with the World Missionary Conference at Edinburgh in 1910.

WATKIN, EDWARD INGRAM. *The Church in council.* New York: Sheed and Ward, 1960. Pp.227. $3.95.

This is a consideration of past general councils and does much to put the reader into the right frame of mind for Vatican II. The author has the rare ability to describe comprehensively and concisely the political and social background for the previous councils.

VII
PASTORAL THEOLOGY

A. GENERAL WORKS

BOUYER, LOUIS, C.Or. *Christian initiation.* New York: Macmillan, 1960. Pp. 148. $3.25.

Father Bouyer deplores the separation which is often made between the spiritual and material world as an impediment to the full development of the human spirit and the integrated Christian life. He suggests that the more conscious man becomes by his own investigations of himself and the universe around him, the more will he be impressed by his role as a Christ-bearer. Hence the reader is led to see Christian truth in confrontation with the world.

CONGAR, YVES, O.P. *Laity, Church and the world.* Translated by D. Attwater. Baltimore, Md.: (Helicon) Taplinger, 1960. Pp. 87. $2.50.

This little book is recommended to all priests for a better understanding of the lay apostolate in our generation.

DAVIS, CHARLES. *Theology for today.* New York: Sheed and Ward, 1962. Pp. 310. $5.00.

In a refreshing way the author argues that theology must be the concern of every mature Christian. There is plenty of food for thought in this book as the author presents the latest scholarship in areas of doctrine such as Christology, Mariology, and the sacraments, and points up their pertinence to everyday life.

FLOOD, PETER, O.S.B. *The priest in practice;* preaching and some other priestly duties. Westminster, Md.: Newman Press, 1962. Pp. 164. $3.50.

Because of his years of experience the author is well equipped to impart sound advice to students, young priests, and even some older ones. About half the book is devoted to preaching in one way or another; the other half discusses such things as ministering to the dying, administration of the other sacraments, and the method of counseling scrupulous people.

GERKEN, JOHN D. *Toward a theology of the layman.* [See page 31.]

*HOLLAND, CORNELIUS JOSEPH. *The shepherd and his flock.* New York: David McKay, 1953. Pp. xi+220. $3.00.

No arm chair philosophizing this. The author is a golden jubilarian with 35 years of experience as a pastor. Not all will agree with his conclusions on pastoral administration, nor does the author touch special problems facing large metropolitan parishes, but his discussions of pastoral zeal, loyalty, and public relations are sound and well written.

KÜNG, HANS. *That the world may believe.* Translated by C. Hastings. New York: Sheed and Ward, 1963. Pp. 149. $3.00.

The tone of this book derives from its genesis, viz., ten letters to a Catholic university student. It is a vademecum for everyone who is in close contact with persons of other faiths.

MICHONNEAU, ABBÉ G. *Revolution in a city parish.* Westminster, Md. Newman Press, 1950. Pp. xxi+189. Pap. $1.50.

Here is a priest who has been successful in developing a really living parish in one of the workers' suburbs of Paris. He sets down in dialogue form the principles—not in the abstract, but as lived—to be followed in the task of making Christ a reality in the pagan world. Throughout there emerges the charity and thirst for souls which permeate the life of the priest-author.

*NAVAGH, JAMES J. *The apostolic parish.* New York: P. J. Kenedy, 1950. Pp. xiii+166. $2.75.

Many attempts are being made to adapt the apostolate to modern times. Although written some years ago, this book is based on the best modern sources of pastoral theology. It can serve as a useful guide, especially for the inexperienced priest, in channeling his various apostolic efforts with a proper method and approach.

*RAHNER, HUGO, S. J. *The parish, from theology to practice.* Translated by R. Cress. Westminster, Md.: Newman Press, 1958. Pp. vii+142. $2.75.

Originally a symposium on the parish, these nine separate essays tend toward the theoretical and speculative. When approached as individual pieces of work, they can and will be greatly rewarding for anyone engaged in the care of souls.

*SELLMAIR, JOSEF. *The priest in the world.* Westminster, Md.: Newman Press, 1954. Pp. x+235. $3.25.

As the title implies, the author is concerned with the diocesan priest. His leading idea is to set forth the right relationship between humanity and mystery in the life of the priest. There are the usual chapters one would expect to find, e.g., on the intellectual and cultural development of the priest, and in addition an exceptionally sound presentation of asceticism and the priest.

VEUILLOT, PIERRE. *The Catholic priesthood, according to the teaching of the Church.* 2v. Westminster, Md.: Newman Press, 1958 and 1964. $7.50 each.

There are times when every priest wants to find out something about the priesthood. These volumes contain every papal statement on the priesthood made since 1903. Its scriptural index, index to the canons, and chronological and analytic indexes make it very usable.

B. HOMILETICS

*COFFIN, HENRY SLOANE. *Communion through preaching.* New York: Scribner's, 1952. Pp. ix+124. $2.50.

This author preserves and emphasizes the ancient interpretation of preaching as "monstrance," with sacramental connotations, and as "event," in which God does something as well as says something.

*DAVIS, HENRY GRADY. *Design for preaching.* Philadelphia: Muhlenberg Press, 1958. Pp. 307. $4.75.

Homiletics related to theology. The Catholic clergy might well learn from their Protestant brethren techniques of constructing good sermons. The author attempts to show how to take a basic truth about God and make it become a living, person-to-person, existential relationship.

FULLER, REGINALD H. *What is liturgical preaching?* Naperville, Ill.: Allenson, 1957. Pp. 64. Pap. $1.50.

The rediscovery of the liturgy has brought with it a rediscovery of the importance of the word in Christian worship. The author writes for the members of the Church of England, but his principles are generally applicable to Roman Catholics.

GIBSON, GEORGE MILES. *Planned preaching.* Philadelphia: Westminster Press, 1954. Pp. 140. $2.50.

Writing in a very informal way, this Protestant author highlights the need for long-range preparation. The book is directed at the veteran of the pulpit as much as at the neophyte.

HITZ, PAUL, C.SS.R. *To preach the Gospel.* Translated by R. Sheed. New York: Sheed and Ward, 1963. Pp. 209. $3.95.

Here the author re-examines the purpose of the preacher and the role of the Christian community. He proposes a return to Christo-centric preaching as an answer to the spiritual needs of the Church today.

JONES, ILION T. *Principles and practice of preaching.* New York: Abingdon Press, 1956. Pp. 272. $3.75.

After consideration of the special role of preaching in the plan of God, the author gives some good, concrete suggestions for the construction of the sermon. In the concluding chapters he gives special attention to the planning and collecting of sermon material.

LISKE, THOMAS V. *Effective preaching.* New York: Macmillan, 1951. Pp. 293. $3.50.

In a direct and human way the author tells his reader how to preach a persuasive sermon by giving some helpful suggestions which pertain to all the elements of the preaching situation: mental attitude, posture, audience contact, the material of the sermon itself, and the delivery. Much information is given on each point and many examples are adduced. Although directed primarily at young priests, this book will be useful to ministers of all denominations and, indeed, to any public speaker.

MACLEOD, DONALD. *Word and sacrament:* a preface to preaching and worship. Englewood Cliffs, N.J.: Prentice-Hall, 1960. Pp. 176. $7.35, text edition, $5.50.

Although the book is written from the viewpoint of the Reformed Churches, Catholics will profit much from it, because it enunciates the principle that preaching itself is worship, and that Word and Sacrament must be combined for perfect worship. Included are a number of illustrative sermons.

MACNUTT, SYLVESTER F., O.P. *Gauging sermon effectiveness.* Dubuque, Iowa: Priory Press, 1960. Pp. 139. Pap. $1.95.

It should be noted that this is not a book on writing inspiring sermons, but on criticizing them. The rules for sermon criticism are neatly explained and illustrated so that the preacher can be his own critic.

MILLER, DONALD G. *The way to biblical preaching.* New York: Abingdon Press, 1957. Pp. 160. $3.00.

The author relates contemporary currents of theology and a deepened interest in the Bible to the minister's weekly preparation of sermons. This is a "how to do it" book for preachers.

PFALLER, LOUIS, O.S.B. *Sermon treasury:* the filing and indexing of sermons and sermon material. Richardton, N. Dak.: Assumption Abbey Press, 1961. Pp. 94. Pap. $1.00.

Every priest has an eye open for sermon materials and may have collected clippings, sermons previously delivered, etc., but their collection is unorganized and inaccessible. This little booklet provides a key to the organization of these materials, so that they can be tapped when needed.

*SANGSTER, WILLIAM E. *The craft of sermon construction.* Philadelphia: Westminster Press, 1951. Pp. 208. $3.00.

A terse and practical work which will serve as a good supplement or extension of the priest's course in homiletics. It is useful and instructive for anyone who feels both the desire and the difficulty of remaining at a reasonably high level in preaching.

STEVENSON, DWIGHT E. *Preaching on the Books of the New Testament.* New York: Harper and Brothers, 1956. Pp. 268. $3.95.

For an understanding of the Bible the faithful need an introduction to each book of the Bible. This and the author's book on the OT, listed below, have been designed as practical manuals for preaching on each book of the Bible.

_____. *Preaching on the Books of the Old Testament.* New York: Harper, 1961. Pp. 267. $3.95.

STRAMBI, VINCENT, SAINT. *Guide to sacred eloquence.* Edited by Pius Leabel, C.P. St. Meinrad, Ind.: Abbey Press, 1963. Pp. 138. Pap. $1.25.

St. Vincent was a student of St. Paul of the Cross. As bishop of Tolentino, in Italy, he distinguished himself in preaching. The first part of the book is a question-answer arrangement which is rapid and effective. There are many good techniques and pointers for success in preaching.

C. CATECHETICS

CASTER, MARCEL VAN, S.J. *The structure of catechetics.* New York: Herder and Herder, 1965. Pp. 253. $4.95.

This is not a book of teaching procedures or classroom techniques for the religion teacher. Rather, it seeks to determine the fundamental methodology of all catechetical instruction on any level. It discusses the fundamentals of catechesis in the light of the current catechetical renewal. The author, who has long been associated with the international catechetical center, *Lumen Vitae,* treats such topics as the nature of catechetics, its threefold function to teach, to form, to initiate, and its various resources: Bible, tradition, anthropology, sociology, and psychology.

A CATHOLIC CATECHISM. New York: Herder and Herder, 1959. Pp. 428. Pap. $1.25.

This is an American edition of the famous German catechism. Its most attractive feature is its use of Scripture. There are questions and answers, but the general style of the book is essay form. The vocabulary and tone of the contents is geared to 7-9 graders.

DOORNIK, N. G. M. VAN. *The meeting with Christ:* a layman's guide to the Catholic faith today. Translated and adapted by J. Paton. New York: P. J. Kenedy, 1964. Pp. xii+237. $4.95.

The subtitle of this book may be a general target label; a more specific designation would be senior high and junior college classes. The fact that it represents the latest in modern Catholic scholarship is evident in the author's use of biblical theology and the concepts of salvation history, and in his emphasis on the Christo-centric life of our faith. About half of the book is concerned with the sacramental life of the Church.

FISCHER, HUBERT, ed. *An introduction to A Catholic Catechism:* its concepts, usage, and aims. New York: Herder and Herder, 1960. Pp. xiv+169. $2.50.

The articles in this little compendium give evidence of the kerygmatic emphasis which is our heritage from apostolic and patristic times. The book will help stimulate a fresh interest in religious instruction.

HILL, JOHN J. and STONE, THEODORE C. *A modern catechism.* Chicago: ACTA Foundation, 1964. Pp. 288.

The contents of this book is comprised of 30 adult-level instructions in the Catholic faith. Each instruction describes an event in salvation history with biblical references to it in the margin. There is also a question and answer section which follows and is meant to help the reader to understand the lesson more clearly. The lessons are divided on principles of modern catechetics. The book is recommended for inquiry classes, adult-education classes and for those engaged in the Newman apostolate.

HOFINGER, JOHANNES, S.J. *The art of teaching Christian doctrine;* the good news and its proclamation. 2d rev. ed. Notre Dame, Ind.: University of Notre Dame Press, 1962. Pp. 290. $4.95.

This is Father Hofinger's latest revision of his major work on modern catechesis. It is a practical work which gets down to the specifics of "what," "how," and "when."

_____. *The Good News yesterday and today.* Translated and edited by W. A. Heusman, S.J. Chicago: Sadlier, 1962. Pp. xii+228. $3.00. Pap. $1.65.

This work first appeared in German in 1936, and is still a key piece in the Church's pastoral renewal. It is one of the first published works of the author. In it he has shown how the liturgical, biblical and catechetical movements coalesce into an organic unity.

_____. *Handing on the faith;* a manual of catechetics. Translated by A. N. Fuerst. New York: Herder and Herder, 1959. Pp. xiv+445. $6.50.

From the second German edition of *Katechetik,* with revisions. As a summing up of this century's progress in catechetics it has no equal in English. Teachers of religion will find it a real treasure.

_____. *Imparting the Christian message;* from the Art of Teaching Christian Doctrine. Notre Dame, Ind.: University of Notre Dame Press, 1962. Pp. 119. Pap. $1.75.

This is an abridged version of the book listed above.

_____, and STONE, THEODORE C. *Pastoral catechetics.* New York: Herder and Herder, 1964. Pp. 287. $4.95.

This is a well-structured collection of 15 articles by various authors on the general theme of a living faith as the goal of religious education. As a collection, this book suffers from the defects of all books that are collections: there is repetition and some unevenness. This aside, however, the articles are enlightening to anyone engaged in religious instruction.

_____, ed. *Teaching all nations:* a symposium on modern catechetics. Revised and translated by C. Howell, S.J. New York: Herder and Herder, 1961. Pp. 421. $6.50.

A symposium on modern catechetics, presenting the papers read at the Conference on Catechetics in Munich, 1960. In general, it stresses a return to biblical catechesis by returning to the form in which the Gospel message was proclaimed. Examples are often lacking; however, some of the papers clearly indicate certain adaptations which might be made in spreading the Good News.

SLOYAN, GERARD S. *Modern catechetics;* message and method in religious formation. New York: Macmillan, 1963. Pp. 379. $5.95.

This is a symposium which embraces some of the best writing on the subject in the English-speaking world. The chapters written by the editor himself are outstanding, especially the one on seminary training. This book is recommended to anyone interested in teaching religion.

_____, ed. *Shaping the Christian message;* essays in religious education. New York: Macmillan, 1958. Pp. 327. $5.95.

In this work 13 experts, experienced in matters of religious education on all levels and in the problems of modern catechetics, gather their insights. Not many real solutions are offered, but the collection succeeds in isolating the problems.

D. MISSIOLOGY

ANDERSON, GERALD H., ed. *The theology of Christian mission.* New York: McGraw-Hill, 1961. Pp. xvii+341. $6.50.

It has become fairly apparent in recent years that the question of the theology of the Christian mission is a question that confronts every religious denomination. Here is a collection of essays, mostly by outstanding Protestant theologians which represent varied approaches to this central question. Few, if any, of these essays will completely carry the assent of the Catholic reader, but all of them could stimulate a greater personal interest in the spread of the Gospel.

CERFAUX, LUCIEN. *Apostle and apostolate, according to the Gospel of St. Matthew.* Translated by D. D. Duggan. New York: Desclee Co., 1960. Pp. 183. $2.75.

This is a commentary on the missionary discourse of our Lord in Matthew 10. In clear and concise language the author reveals the spiritual riches of Christ's missionary exhortations, and shows how they have been realized in the lives of saints like Francis of Assisi, Benedict Joseph Labre, and John Vianney.

DANIÉLOU, JEAN, S.J. *The advent of salvation.* Translated by R. Sheed. Glen Rock, N. J.: Paulist Press, 1962. Pp. 192. Pap. $0.95.

By studying the relationship of non-Christian religions to Catholicism, the author hopes to contribute to the formation of a sound missionary spirituality. For the author, the Christian Gospel is the fulfillment and perfection of the pagan preparations which preceded it.

_____. *The salvation of the nations.* Translated by A. Bouchard. Notre Dame, Ind.: University of Notre Dame Press, 1962. Pp. 118. Pap. $1.75.

The aim of this book is the cultivation of a genuine missionary spirituality through broadening and deepening the missionary perspective. Mission work is the extension and prolongation of the Word Incarnate, and must render Christianity incarnate in all nations and peoples.

HENRY, ANTONIN M., O.P. *A mission theology.* Translated by A. J. Le-Mothe. Notre Dame, Ind.: Fides Publishers, 1963. Pp. 197. $3.95. (Themes of theology)

A recurrent theme of this book is that the Christian community is in some sense to blame for the lack of faith which surrounds it, because the spread of faith depends on the vitality of the new commandment of fraternal love. The Church is missionary even when the faith is firmly planted, for Christian life is a continuous conversion.

HITZ, PAUL, C.SS.R. *To preach the Gospel.* [See page 93.]

HOFINGER, JOHANNES, S.J. *Worship: the life of the missions.* Notre Dame, Ind.: University of Notre Dame Press, 1958. Pp. 337. $6.00.

A thought-provoking piece of reasoned argumentation for liturgical reform with a view to the missions. The editor finds that the earlier and simpler forms of worship were molded by the needs of a missionary Church.

McCOY, JOSEPH A., S.M. *Advice from the field.* Baltimore, Md.: (Helicon) Taplinger, 1962. Pp. 288. $4.95.

Although this work was originally a doctrinal dissertation, it is valuable to the general reader insofar as it isolates some of the problems of American missionaries. The chief of these problems seems to be the lack of pre-departure training. This work shows a tendency to oversimplification, for it largely overlooks missiology as a science.

MILLOT, RENÉ PIERRE. *Missions in the world today.* Translated by J. H. Smith. New York: Hawthorn Books, 1961. Pp. 139. $3.50. (Twentieth century encyclopedia of Catholicism, 100)

This work stresses some special characteristics of modern missions and presents some startling statistical accounting. The author manages to convey his deep understanding of missionary problems.

MISSIOLOGY IN AFRICA TODAY; thought-provoking essays by modern missionaries. Edited by Desmond J. Hatton. Dublin: M. H. Gill, 1961. Pp. 151. $0.85.

The editor definitely has Africa in his mind, but he has taken care not to exclude the missionary world in general. He has selected and arranged his material under four specific headings: General; Sociological; Methods and Means; and Specific Mission.

MURPHY, EDWARD L., S.J. *Teach ye all nations;* the principles of Catholic missionary work. New York: Benziger Brothers, 1958. Pp. 234. $3.50.

A useful work as a source of dogmatic and historical information on Catholic missionary work. The author holds the degree of Doctor of Missiology from the Gregorian University in Rome. Perhaps his most powerful and moving chapter is the one on supranationalism and adaptation.

RÉTIF, LOUIS and RÉTIF, ANDRÉ. *The Church's mission in the world.* Translated by R. F. Trevett. New York: Hawthorn Books, 1962. Pp. 156. $3.50. (Twentieth century encyclopedia of Catholicism, 102)

The message of the Rétif brothers is this: in matters pertaining to the missions we must think big and think fast. The authors stress the fact that missionary work is not primarily philanthropic, social, cultural or civilizing, but must primarily be salvific.

*ROCHE, ALOYSIUS. *In the track of the Gospel;* an outline of the Christian apostolate from Pentecost to the present. New York: P. J. Kenedy, 1953. Pp. 200. $3.00.

This is not a treatise on missiology as such, but rather a history of the spread of the Gospel during the past nineteen centuries. Although the book is short, the author has succeeded in placing a proper emphasis and in being surprisingly detailed at times. Of special interest is his attention to the role which women have played in the history of the missions.

SUENENS, LEON JOSEPH CARDINAL. *The Gospel to every creature.* With a preface by John Baptist Montini. Translated by L. G. Duffy. Westminster, Md.: Newman Press, 1957. Pp. 163. Pap. $1.75.

This book is geared to inspire Christians to become what they are. The author has done much to stir Catholics from their lethargy and to make them realize their obligations in spreading the kingdom of God. He discusses such problems as "to humanize or to evangelize," the oneness of the priestly apostolate and the lay apostolate, and methods of preparation for the apostolate. Some of his statements are shocking because they are true.

VAULX, BERNARD DE. *History of the missions.* Translated by R. F. Trevett. New York: Hawthorn Books, 1961. Pp. 191. $3.50. (Twentieth century encyclopedia of Catholicism, 49)

A brief and competent survey of the history of the Church's missionary effort from the time of the Apostles to Benedict XV. There is nothing about the modern situation, nor about the much discussed questions of adaptation. Within these limits, it is a useful book for reference and background information.

VIII
PASTORAL PSYCHOLOGY AND COUNSELING*

ACKERMANN, NATHAN W. *The psychodynamics of family life.* New York: Basic Books, 1958. Pp. 379. $6.75.

This is a valuable resource for those who are thinking seriously about any kind of educational, counseling or therapeutic intervention in the family process. "It presents a way of understanding health in the 'emotional give and take' of family relationships. It outlines the conceptual approach to emotional disturbance in the individual through analysis of the psychological content of his family experience" (Preface).

BIER, WILLIAM CHRISTIAN, S.J. *The adolescent:* his search for understanding. New York: Fordham University Press, 1963. Pp. 246. $5.00. (Pastoral Psychology, 3)

This book is composed of 24 papers presented during the 1961 Fordham University Institute of Pastoral Psychology. It's editor is a respected priest-psychologist.

BLOOD, ROBERT O., Jr., and WOLFE, DONALD M. *Husbands and wives;* the dynamics of married living. Glencoe, Ill.: Free Press, 1960. Pp. 293. $5.95.

This is one of the more recent sociological analyses of the relationship between husband and wife. It covers a variety of subjects, from decision making and economic functions of the family to love and emotional well-being. The material for the book was gathered from questionnaires to married couples. It is good from the sociological point of view, but lacks some of the more dynamic interpretation that a counselor would want.

BLOS, PETER. *On Adolescence.* Glencoe, Ill.: Free Press, 1963. Pp. 269. $5.95.

Dr. Blos describes clearly the stages of adolescent development, not only in theoretical terms, but with ample case material. The phases of development are unified by the concept of the self as it progresses and is consolidated during adolescence.

BOISEN, ANTON T. *The exploration of the inner world.* New York: Harper and Row, 1936. Pp. xi+322. $1.75.

---

*The scope, limits and functions of pastoral counseling are not, as yet, clearly defined. One thing is clear: the pastor has much to learn from the fields of psychiatry, psychology and social work. The task of integrating knowledge from these fields with the work of the ministry is the progressive and collective task of those who intend to be helpful via counseling relationships. The selections of this chapter are offered as a basis for integration. The list is broadly interdisciplinary and frankly ecumenical. We wish to express our gratitude for the preparation of this section to Dr. Seward Hiltner, Professor of Theology and Personality, Princeton Theological Seminary and Dr. Donald Young, Director of the Pastoral Care and Counseling Program, The Menninger Foundation.

—Aquinas Sipe, O.S.B., Topeka, Kansas.

The founder of the modern movement for clinical education of the clergy presents in this volume the basic thesis that led him to posit a relationship between certain forms of religious experience and certain forms of mental disorder. It was in this way that he perceived how pastors, studying under supervision while ministering to the mentally ill, could improve their pastoral insight and deepen their theological insight at the same time.

BRISTER, C. W. *Pastoral care in the Church.* New York: Harper and Row, 1964. Pp. xxiv+262. $5.00.

A Baptist minister and pastoral theologian examine ways in which new insights into pastoral care, through both psychology and theology, may be practically put to work in the regular ministry of the local parish.

*CABOT, RICHARD C. and DICKS, RUSSELL L. *The art of ministering to the sick.* New York: Macmillan, 1936. Pp. viii+384. $3.00.

One of the early classics in the modern Protestant rediscovery of pastoral care, this volume, by a distinguished physician and a hospital chaplain, gives much useful information about pastoral approach to the sick patient, and argues effectively for a discriminating use of pastoral time with persons most needing pastoral help. Although dated in a few particulars, its thrust is still highly useful.

CAVANAGH, JOHN R. *Fundamental marriage counseling.* Milwaukee: Bruce, 1957. Pp. 598. $8.00.

This manual assembles a large number of facts which the author feels will be needed by one concerned with preserving the integrity of the marriage relationship. The text is weighted with medical material, but also contains contributions by specialists in the fields of sociology and religion. The effectiveness of the book may be limited by a somewhat biased thesis.

CLEBSCH, WILLIAM and JAEKLE, CHARLES. *Pastoral care in historical perspective.* Englewood Cliffs, N. J.: Prentice-Hall, 1964. Pp. 344. $7.95.

By a Protestant church historian and pastoral theologian, this volume begins with a constructive modern statement of major modes of pastoral care (healing, sustaining, guiding, reconciling), argues that each major epoch in the Church's history has used one of these as focal, and thus sets the modern situation imaginatively in historical context. The text occupies a third of the book, the remainder being an excellent selection of illustrative historical documents from the whole history of Christian pastoral care, thoughtfully annotated.

CURRAN, CHARLES A. *Counseling in Catholic life and education.* New York: Macmillan, 1952. Pp. xxvi+462. $10.60, text edition $7.95.

This far-reaching volume by a priest-psychologist begins with St. Thomas's distinction between "counsel" and "guidance," expounds the significance of the priest's alertness to the inner individuality of the person in the stage of "counsel," and presents many case illustrations of actual procedure and grounds for the procedure, considered both psychologically and theologically.

DUVALL, E. *Love and the facts of life.* New York: Association Press, 1963. Pp. 352. $4.95.

Good books on sex are hard to find. This volume does not end the search. In many respects it is more adequate than many; however, Catholic adolescents may be confused by the author's treatment of purity.

EMERSON, JAMES GORDON, Jr. *The dynamics of forgiveness.* Philadelphia: Westminster Press, 1964. Pp. 203. $5.00.

A Presbyterian minister and pastoral theologian argues that forgiveness, as the heart of the Gospel, is also the proper central focus for pastoral care in the local church or parish. Employing historical as well as contemporary analysis, he argues that forgiveness is misunderstood unless it includes both "context" (God's making it available through grace) and "instrumentation" (the "means of grace," however interpreted).

ENGLISH, O. SPURGEON and PEARSON, GERALD H. J. *Emotional problems of living.* Rev. ed. New York: W. W. Norton, 1955. Pp. 592. $7.50, text edition $5.65.

This is one of the best single-volume works on personality development. Ranging from infancy through the problems of aging, it yields helpful insights on the stages of development. In addition to outlining the developmental stages, it also discusses the emotional difficulties often seen in each stage. It is a good companion to Saul's *Emotional Maturity,* which deals primarily with the dynamics of personality.

ERIKSON, ERIK. *Childhood and society.* Rev. ed. New York: W. W. Norton, 1963. Pp. 445. $6.50.

This book can be considered one of the classics in the study of the social significance of childhood. The author provides a broad base for the understanding of human beings with clarity, penetration, and humor.

GASSERT, R. and HALL, B. *Psychiatry and religious faith.* New York: Viking Press, 1964. Pp. xx+171. $3.95.

A priest and psychiatrist collaborate to provide a basic primer for those who are tempted to think religion and psychiatry are incompatible. They succeed in clarifying some common misconceptions.

GOLDBRUNNER, JOSEPH. *Cure of mind and cure of soul.* New York: Pantheon, 1958. Pp. 127. $2.75. Pap. $0.95.

The title is the author's thesis. The more we seek perfection which makes man like God, the more we can become healthy in body and soul, for holiness is health. The author is a priest, theologian, and psychologist.

HAGMAIER, GEORGE, C.S.P. and GLEASON, ROBERT W., S.J. *Counseling the Catholic.* New York: Sheed and Ward, 1959. Pp. xiv+301. $4.50.

The emotional stratum of a man's life is the focal point of interest for the Paulist and Jesuit collaborators. Their aim is to help priests and seminarians build new attitudes based on the findings of modern psychology. They communicate their message with lucidity, directness, and expertise.

HILTNER, SEWARD. *The Christian shepherd.* New York: Abingdon Press, 1959. Pp. 190. $4.00.

There is much in common in pastoral counseling for Protestant and Catholic clergymen, and therefore the priest can learn much from this book. It will greatly help him improve his personal effectiveness in the ministry of counseling.

_____. *Pastoral counseling.* New York: Abingdon Press, 1949. Pp. 291. $3.00.

Considers pastoral counseling as one aspect of the ministry of pastoral care and therefore as part of the function of every clergyman. It also emphasizes the relationship between basic principles and concrete practice, and presents and analyzes many concrete situations. Andre Godin, S.J. has said that the Catholic reader need make allowances in the author's discussion of religious resources for pastoral counseling.

————. *Preface to pastoral theology.* New York: Abingdon Press, 1958. Pp. 240. $4.00.

An effort to reconsider the diffuse meanings that "pastoral theology" has had in Protestantism. It argues for pastoral theology conceived as theological theory related to concrete pastoral practice. To provide a context for pastoral theology as one of the "function-oriented" branches of theology, the book proposes an alternative structure to the traditional offices of the church and ministry.

————. *The adolescent and his world.* New York: Family Service Association of America, 1952. Pp. 124. Pap. $1.75.

The present volume grew out of the popularity of Dr. Josselyn's earlier work, *Psychosocial Development of Children.* Like that volume, it is reliable, sensitively written and focused for those who are working in close interpersonal relationships with adolescents. It is not a primer, however, and should not be read without some earlier work and study in the area of adolescent personality development.

*JOSSELYN, IRENE M. *Psychosocial development of children.* New York: Family Service Association of America, 1948. Pp. 134. Pap. $1.75.

A very helpful paperback volume that resulted from a course for social workers sponsored by the Family Service Association of America. It is an excellent and sensitively written volume on the psychological-social development of children.

McCANN, RICHARD V. *The churches and mental health.* New York: Basic Books, 1962. Pp. 227. $6.00.

Part of a 10-volume series issued by the Joint Commission on Mental Illness and Health. This volume is directly and objectively concerned with learning what resources for mental health religion makes available to people. Religion is here taken primarily as represented by a certain affiliation to a church and its clergy.

*McNEILL, JOHN T. *A history of the cure of souls.* New York: Harper and Row, 1951. Pp. 371. $5.00.

This is quite a monumental work on the subject, for the author runs almost the complete gamut of Christian and Oriental cultures and their concern for the healing of souls.

*MAVES, PAUL B. and CEDERLEAF, J. LENNART. *Older people and the Church.* New York: Abingdon Press, 1949. Pp. 272. $2.50.

This work reports on a research study of pastoral care to a selected population of older people, and on companion studies dealing with programs for older people in selected Protestant parishes. In addition, it summarizes recent findings about older people in our society and about the nature of the aging process.

MENNINGER, KARL. *The vital balance.* New York: Viking Press, 1964. Pp. 531. $10.00.

These pages are filled with wisdom, balance and plain good sense. The author believes that psychiatry should be providing a better understanding of human beings, well and sick, without labeling them pejoratively. Aiming at a dynamic description which will be accurate, useful, and intelligible to those concerned with human beings, the book makes mental health and mental illness make sense.

OATES, WAYNE E., ed. *Introduction to pastoral counseling.* Nashville: Broadman Press, 1959. Pp. 331. $6.00.

Professors of pastoral care in the several seminaries of the Southern Baptist Convention join here in providing a basic textbook for their students. Most of the chapters are of good quality, and the entire volume is ecumenical in its outlook.

ORAISON, MARC. *Love or constraint?* Translated by U. Morrissy. New York: P. J. Kenedy, 1959. Pp. 172. Pap. $0.95.

This book is specifically directed at those concerned with the psychology and philosophy of religious education. The author advocates encouraging children as far as is humanly possible to those potentialities that will become, under the action of God, the theological virtues.

PERLMAN, HELEN HARRIS. *Social casework;* a problem solving process. Chicago: University of Chicago Press, 1957. Pp. 268. $5.00.

Although this book is written primarily for social case workers, it is an excellent volume for the clergyman who wants to think systematically about his own pastoral counseling. The author outlines carefully the components of the case work (pastoral counseling) situation in a very sensitive way. The book gives particular stress to the beginning phase of the counseling process. This should be a valuable resource for pastoral counselors because of the importance of the initial contacts with parishioners, which largely determine the direction of the counseling process.

SAUL, LEON J. *Emotional maturity.* Philadelphia: J. P. Lippincott, 1947. Pp. xii+338. $7.50.

This is one of the earlier books on psychodynamics. It is an excellent and easily understood reference on personality development and function. It deals with such subjects as dependence, the need for love, hostility, and has a very helpful section on the nature of neurosis.

SNOECK, ANDRE, S.J. *Confession and pastoral psychology.* Translated by T. Zuydwijk. Westminster, Md.: Newman Press, 1961. Pp. 183. $3.50.

The author does a good job of maintaining a clear distinction between the sacrament of penance and the science of psychology, yet he urges confessors to use psychology to avoid errors. Almost half of the book is devoted to pastoral care of a scrupulous person.

WISE, CARROLL A. *Pastoral counseling:* its theory and practice. New York: Harper and Row, 1951. Pp. 231. $2.75.

Practical aspects of pastoral work and counseling are considered in detail, but the essence of counseling is presented as communication, which is a two-way process deeper than verbal expression, in which the whole personality participates in a therapeutic relationship.

YOUNG, RICHARD K. and MEIBURG, ALBERT L. *Spiritual therapy.* New York: Harper and Row, 1960. Pp. 184. $3.50.

Two Protestant hospital chaplains present general observations on various major types of physical illness, with pastoral suggestions on how ministry to each type may be made more relevant. The book's unhappy title should not be permitted to mislead readers concerning the competent, though introductory, content.

IX
PASTORAL SOCIOLOGY

BERELSON, BERNARD, ed. *The behavioral sciences today.* New York: Basic Books, 1963. Pp. 275. $4.95. Pap. Harper Torchbks (Tb1127) $1.75.

This is a collection of papers originally given as a series of talks in the Forum series of The Voice in America. The papers are generally excellent, clearly presented, and stimulating. They give a good over-view of their subject.

DUFF, EDWARD, S.J. *The social thought of the World Council of Churches.* [See page 62.]

EMERY, EDWIN, and others. *Introduction to mass communications.* New York: Dodd, Mead, 1960. Pp. xii+435. $6.00.

Designed as a college text, this book does a fine job of giving the reader a comprehensive picture of the mass media upon which he depends as a citizen. It is virtually required reading for those who want to be informed consumers of what the mass media have to offer.

FICHTER, JOSEPH HENRY, S.J. *Parochial school,* a sociological study. Notre Dame, Ind.: University of Notre Dame Press, 1958. Pp. 495. $6.00.

This work is the result of a year-long survey made by a team of 10 graduate students of sociology, under the direction of the author. The research was conducted in South Bend, Ind. As a scientific observation removed from theorizing and guesswork, this is a significant contribution in that it presents a descriptive study of the operation of a parochial school. The reader is led to infer that the parochial school is a substantial success as an American institution.

_____. *Social relations in the urban parish.* Chicago: University of Chicago Press, 1954. Pp. 263. $5.50.

Father Fichter is a sober, well-informed sociologist, and his book is a realistic appraisal of a parish. Written in scholarly form, its basic purpose is to get pastors and other readers to face sociological facts.

GLAZER, NATHAN and MOYNIHAN, DANIEL PATRICK. *Beyond the melting pot;* the Negroes, Puerto Ricans, Jews, Italians, and Irish of New York City. Cambridge, Mass.: M. I. T. Press, 1963. Pp. vii+360. $7.50. Pap. $1.95.

This is an intelligent book on a subject surrounded by taboos. It suggests that, contrary to our beliefs and/or hopes, the American never really melted down, and that ethnic lines are stronger today than ever. The book might offend partisans, but it springs from knowledge and love.

GREELEY, ANDREW. *Religion and career.* New York: Sheed and Ward, 1963. Pp. 267. $5.00.

This is an impressive study by a priest-sociologist of the influence of religion upon the career and graduate school plans of the nation's college graduates of June, 1961. The conclusion serves as documentation for the apparent recent rise in the status of American Catholics.

GUERRY, EMILE MAURICE. *The social doctrine of the Catholic Church.* Translated by M. Hederman. New York: Alba House, 1962. Pp. 287. $4.95.

The author is the archbishop of Cambrai, France. In this book he accomplishes his objective of showing what things are to be believed, what to be acted upon, and what are the values to be used as norms in the Church's teachings about employer and employee.

HAUSER, PHILIP M. *Population perspectives.* New Brunswick, N. J.: Rutgers University Press, 1960. Pp. 183. $3.50.

The perspectives given are both sociologically informed and refreshingly different. The last chapter proposes some concrete suggestions. The factual basis of the author's conclusions are unassailable, and eye-opening for many.

HUFF, DARRELL. *How to lie with statistics.* New York: W. W. Norton, 1954. Pp. 142. $3.50. Pap. $1.95.

Anyone who reads this book will be better qualified to evaluate statistical data, and will be more on his guard against the false impressions which can be conveyed by statistics. While this is a cautionary book, it also imparts much knowledge about the fundamentals of the science of statistics.

LERNER, DANIEL, ed. *The human meaning of the social sciences.* New York: Peter Smith, 1959. Pp. 317. $3.50. Pap. Meridian (M64) $1.55.

The editor is professor of sociology and international communication at M.I.T. In the first part of the book he gives its scope in a chapter entitled "Social Science: whence and whither." The following chapters are under the headings: Retrospect, Issues, Uses, and Prospects. The contributors include notable sociologists like Nathan Glazer, Harold Lasswell, Clyde Kluckhohn and Margaret Mead, who are dedicated to the proposition that social science is more than a peculiar new vocabulary. To illustrate this they show the close relationship between social change and social research.

McCORMACK, ARTHUR, S.M.S.J., ed. *Christian responsibility and world poverty.* Westminster, Md.: Newman Press, 1963. Pp. xiii+314. $6.50.

A collection of 19 papers originally written by various prominent personages that are well-known for their interest and effort to improve human welfare. Some of the questions discussed are world poverty, underdevelopment and population; marriage and responsible parenthood; the communist and Catholic solutions; the agricultural and economic revolution; India, South America and Africa; Christian responsibility and international social justice.

MOODY, JOSEPH N. and LAWLER, JUSTUS GEORGE, edd. *The challenge of Mater et Magistra.* New York: Herder and Herder, 1963. Pp. vii+280. $4.95.

This commentary on the encyclical begins with an historical study of Catholic social thought; it also contains five essays on various themes of the encyclical. It has been criticized, in that the essays are too independent of each other, but in spite of this flaw it is a welcome English commentary on the encyclical.

SCHUYLER, JOSEPH B., S.J. *Northern parish;* a sociological and pastoral study. Chicago: Loyola University Press, 1960. Pp. xxi+360. $8.00.

A highly documented survey of Our Lady of Mercy Parish in the Bronx, New York City. It aims to suggest possible reasons for various observed uniformities and divergencies in religious practice. It will help the priest and the intellectual layman gain some appreciation of the value of visualizing the parish scientifically as a social unit.

THOMAS, JOHN L., S.J. *The American Catholic family.* Englewood Cliffs, N.J.: Prentice-Hall, 1956. Pp. 471. $11.35, text edition $8.50.

Father Thomas writes like the sociologist that he is. In discussing the American family, he bases his observations not on theoretical guesses, but on empirical data. The book develops in three sections: the Catholic concept of marriage; the description of family breakdown; programs for survival.

VIDICH, ARTHUR J. and BENSMAN, JOSEPH. *Small town in mass society.* New York: Peter Smith, 1960. Pp. 337. $3.50. Pap. Anchor (A216) $1.45.

"The small town" of this study by two young sociologists is Springdale, in upstate New York. This is an eminently readable report of the impact of a larger society on the ideas, opinions, and actions of the small community.

WACH, JOACHIM. *Sociology of religion.* Chicago: University of Chicago Press, 1944. Pp. 418. Pap. Phoenix (P92) $1.95.

Probably the best work on the sociology of religion. It must be remembered that it is a scientific work on sociology, so the reader should not turn to it to find a discussion of, say, the intrinsic supernatural character of the Church. In this treatment, the Church is simply considered as one of many types of religious bodies.

WHYTE, WILLIAM H. *The organization man.* New York: Simon and Schuster, 1956. Pp. 429. $5.00. Pap. Anchor (A117) $1.45.

The author points out the trend of a new ethic, that of groupism as opposed to individualism. His thesis is that the organization ethic is static, delusory, and self-destructive. These are thought-provoking reflections on modern society.

X
CHRISTIAN ART AND ARCHITECTURE

CHRIST-JANIER, ALBERT and FOLEY, MARY MIX. *Modern church architecture.* New York: McGraw-Hill, 1962. Pp. 333. $9.75.

The section on Catholic churches discusses the liturgical revival and encourages new architectural concepts which will provide liturgical orientation. Each denomination is treated separately, and in many instances there are informative statements by the clergy.

DAVIES, JOHN GORDON. *The origin and development of early Christian church architecture.* Naperville, Ill.: Allenson, 1952. Pp. xiii+152. $4.50.

This is truly a contribution to the field because it covers ground not previously touched in modern English treatises. It has been warmly welcomed by students of architecture and by those interested in the origins of church buildings.

*DILLISTONE, FREDERICK W. *Christianity and symbolism.* Philadelphia: Westminster Press, 1955. Pp. 320. $4.50.

This subject is currently receiving great attention. When the author speaks of Christianity and symbolism in general, he does so in a masterful way. In speaking of symbolism in the sacraments, however, there could be a greater theological depth.

GETLEIN, FRANK and GETLEIN, DOROTHY. *Christianity in art.* Milwaukee: Bruce, 1959. Pp. 196. $4.50.

An interesting thesis is the point of departure for these two collaborators: the varying relationships between Church and State are intimately bound up with the development of Christian art. The authors are at their best in helping the reader understand how the great artists have employed line, color, and mass in their composition.

_____. *Christianity and modern art.* Milwaukee: Bruce, 1961. Pp. xiii+227. $5.00.

The author-critics are not writing for other critics in hermetic code or jargon; they speak openly and straightforwardly to the ordinary adult. This honest and charitable book should help to restore the role of the Church as patron of the arts.

GILSON, ETIENNE. *The arts of the beautiful.* New York: Scribner's, 1965. Pp. 192. $4.50.

The latest publication of the famous French philosopher in which he makes a clear statement on what he takes to be the nature of the fine arts. Contrary to popular belief, Gilson argues that art is not the expression of the artist himself or his vision of reality, but only a kind of making, namely the making of a thing of beauty which has its own intrinsic value. The book combines the insights of a renowned historian of philosophy with the living experience of a modern man.

GOUGH, MICHAEL. *The early Christians.* New York: Praeger, 1961. Pp. 268. $7.50.

The author's field of study is early Christian archeology. In this book he takes us back to the age of Justinian. While his work is an historical survey, it is mainly concerned with the development of early Christian art and the evolution of the early Christian house of worship.

HAMMOND, PETER. *Liturgy and architecture.* New York: Columbia University Press, 1961. Pp. xv+191. $6.00.

This book, coming from an Anglican clergyman, is evidence of how the liturgical movement has influenced Protestants. Here he applies the principles of liturgy to church building.

_____, ed. *Towards a church architecture.* London: Architectural Press, 1962. Pp. 262. $6.00.

This book laments the opportunities which have been wasted by church architecture in the past. Its basic message is that since problems of church design are more fundamentally problems of the nature of the Church itself, church architecture should be adapted to the exigencies of the liturgy.

*HENZE, ANTON and FILTHAUT, THEODOR. *Contemporary church art.* Translated by C. Hastings. New York: Sheed and Ward, 1956. Pp. 64+128. $7.50.

The message of this clear but provocative work is that we rid ourselves of the 19th century concept of church art and get back to the traditional idea that the sacred artist is a man who makes all things needed in the house of God. It is practical in outlining the role of the patron of art or architecture.

LEEUW, GERARDUS VAN DER. *Sacred and profane beauty:* the holy in art. Translated by E. E. Green. New York: Holt, Rinehart, and Winston, 1963. Pp. xx+357. $6.50.

Originally written in Dutch, the English text is a translation from the German version. The author's concern is to point up the contact between the holy and the beautiful. Besides art and architecture, he treats other forms of art such as dance, drama, music and painting. The last chapter is a discussion of theological aesthetics.

LESAGE, ROBERT. *Vestments and church furniture.* Translated by F. Murphy. New York: Hawthorn Books, 1960. Pp. 152. $3.50. (Twentieth century encyclopedia of Catholicism, 114)

The topics summarized by the author include the altar, crucifix, sacred vessels, bells, lighting, liturgical books, fonts, vessels and clerical costume. The treatment is concise, clear and free of uninteresting details.

*MÂLE, ÉMILE. *The early churches of Rome.* Translated by D. Buxton. Chicago: Quadrangle Books, 1960. Pp. 253. $12.50.

This study deals with the most interesting early Christian and Medieval churches of Rome in a roughly chronological sequence from the first to the 13th centuries. Together with its 64 pages of photographs, it contains a wealth of information on the history of church art and architecture.

_____. *Religious art:* from the twelfth to the eighteenth century. New York: Noonday Press, 1963. Pp. 208. Pap. $1.75.

The author's writings are considered classics of scholarly achievement. This work is a condensation of many of his other writings. It is written in a style that combines eloquence with power and authority of the author. It portrays the grandeur of the artistic renaissance that accompanied the Counter-Reformation.

MARITAIN, JACQUES. *The responsibility of the artist.* New York: Scribner's, 1960. Pp. 120. $2.95.

At a time when many are being afflicted with an artistic irresponsibility, Maritain's book might sound anachronistic. Actually it is very relevant and profound in presenting the moral dimensions of the artistic enterprise. Its four essays are entitled: Art and Morality; Art for Art's Sake; Art for the People; and Poetry and Perfection of Human Life.

*MILLS, EDWARD DAVID. *The modern church.* New York: Praeger, 1956. Pp. 188. $9.75.

Since it treats of the design and construction of contemporary churches, this is a practical book. The author, an experienced London architect, also examines present-day trends in the arrangement of church interiors.

RÉGAMEY, RAYMOND, O.P. *Religious art in the twentieth century.* New York: Herder and Herder, 1963. Pp. 256. $4.95.

This book has been hailed as a *summa* of sound artistic sense. Its strongest virtue is its refusal to canonize any single artistic style as the right one. There are many mansions in the house of Christian art, and we must never presume to grasp one, nor to exclude the possibility of many more in the future.

RICE, DAVID TALBOT. *The beginnings of Christian art.* New York: Abingdon Press, 1958. Pp. 223. $7.95.

Since the author's scope is so comprehensive, this work will be useful in helping the interested reader understand subsequent art developments. He includes the first seven centuries of Christian art, also the development of Byzantine art, and sketches of the Carolingian and Ottonian periods.

SCHWARZ, RUDOLF. *The Church incarnate;* the sacred function of Christian architecture. Translated by C. Harris. Chicago: H. Regnery Co., 1958. Pp. 231. $10.00.

Here the author is groping to express his insights, not on architecture as such, but rather on the sacred space contained therein — the space where the Christian sacrificial cult takes place. It is not easy reading, for the reader must bring an understanding of theology as well as of art.

SEASOLTZ, R. KEVIN, O.S.B. *The house of God;* sacred art and church architecture. New York: Herder and Herder, 1963. Pp. 272. $4.95.

It is a genuine help to have a book like this one to guide us in formulating our basic concepts on liturgical art. The author's norms are based on his interpretation of the Code of Canon Law, and the instruction *De Arte Sacra.*

SMITH, G. E. KIDDER. *The new churches of Europe.* New York: Holt, Rinehart and Winston, 1964. Pp. 291. $17.50.

The author is a major architectural historian and photographer who has selected 60 of the greatest post-war churches by architects such as Le Corbusier, Aalto, and Schwarz. There are over 500 photographs and about half as many line drawings which illustrate the author's sensitive and authoritative comments.

SYNDICUS, EDUARD. *Early Christian art.* Translated by J. R. Foster. New York: Hawthorn Books, 1962. Pp. 188. $3.50. (Twentieth century encyclopedia of Catholicism, 121)

There is a lot of information in this little book. Not only does the author show evidence of a good grasp of the art under consideration, but he also shows evidence of a theological mentality able to relate art to the historical period which conceived it.

AUTHOR INDEX

PUBLISHERS ADDRESSES

The following list of publishers' addresses is provided for those who do not have access to a local bookstore.

Abbey Press
[*See* Grail Publications]

Abingdon Press
55 E. 55th St.
New York 22, N.Y.

ACTA Foundation
1655 W. Jackson Blvd.
Chicago, Ill.

Alba House
2187 Victory Blvd.
Staten Island 14, N.Y.

Aldine Publishing Co.
64 E. Van Buren St.
Chicago 5, Ill.

Allen & Unwin
Ruskin House
40 Museum St.
London, W.C. 1, England

Alec E. Allenson, Inc.
635 E. Ogden Av.
Naperville, Ill.

American Schools of Oriental Research
Drawer 93A-Yale Station
New Haven, Conn.

Architectural Press, Ltd.
9-13 Queen Anne's Gate
Westminster
London, S.W. 1, England

Arts Inc. Publishers
667 Madison Ave.
New York 21, N.Y.

Association Press
291 Broadway
New York 21, N.Y.

Assumption Abbey Press
Richardton, N. Dak.

Augsburg Publishing House
426 S. 5th St.
Minneapolis 15, Minn.

Barnes & Noble, Inc.
105 5th Ave.
New York 3, N.Y.

Basic Books, Inc.
404 Park Ave. S.
New York 16, N.Y.

Belknap Press
[*See* Harvard Univ. Press]

Benziger Brothers, Inc.
7 E. 51st St.
New York 22, N.Y.

Geoffry Bles, Ltd.
52 Doughty St.
London W.C. 1, England

Charles T. Branford Co.
75 Union St.
Newton Centre 59, Mass.

E. J. Brill
Oude Rijn
33a-35, Leiden, Netherlands

British Book Centre
122 E. 55th St.
New York 22, N.Y.

The Broadman Press
127 9th Ave. N.
Nashville, Tenn.

Brown & Nolan, Ltd.
Clonskeagh
Dublin 4, Ireland

Bruce Publishing Co.
400 N. Broadway
Milwaukee 1, Wis.

Burns & Oates
25 Ashley Pl.
London S.W. 1, England

Cahill & Co.
Parkgate St.
Dublin, Ireland

Cambridge Univ. Press
32 E. 57th St.
New York 22, N.Y.

Catholic Hospital Assn. of U.S. & Canada
1438 S. Grand Blvd.
St. Louis 4, Mo.

Catholic Univ. of America Press
620 Michigan Ave. N.E
Washington 17, D.C.

Challoner Publications, Ltd.
Tenbury Wells
Worcestershire, England

Collier Books
60 5th Ave.
New York 11, N.Y.

Columbia Univ. Press
2960 Broadway
New York 27, N.Y.

Cornell Univ. Press
124 Roberts Pl.
Ithaca, N.Y.

Thomas Y. Crowell Co.
201 Park Ave. S.
New York 3, N.Y.

Dacre
  [See Macmillan]

Desclee Co., Inc.
280 Broadway
New York 7, N.Y.

Dodd Mead & Co.
432 Park Ave. S.
New York 16, N.Y.

Doubleday & Co.
501 Franklin Ave.
Garden City, N.Y.

E. P. Dutton & Co.
201 Park Ave. S.
New York 3, N.Y.

Wm. B. Eerdmans Publishing Co.
255 Jefferson Ave. S.E.
Grand Rapids 3, Mich.

Family Service Assoc. of America
44 E. 23d St.
New York 10, N.Y.

Farrar, Straus & Co.
19 Union Sq. W.
New York 3, N.Y.

Fides Publishers
Box 38
Notre Dame, Ind.

Fordham Univ. Press
441 E. Fordham Rd.
New York 58, N.Y.

The Free Press of Glencoe
60 5th Ave.
New York 11, N.Y.

M. H. Gill & Sons
50 Upper O'Connell St.
Dublin 1, Ireland

Grail Publications
St. Meinrad, Ind.

Grove Press, Inc.
64 University Pl.
New York 3, N.Y.

Hanover House
  [See Doubleday]

Harcourt, Brace & World, Inc.
750 3rd Ave.
New York 17, N.Y.

Harper & Row Publishers
49 E. 33rd St.
New York 16, N.Y.

Harvard Univ. Press
Kittredge Hall
79 Garden St.
Cambridge 38, Mass.

Hawthorn Books, Inc.
70 5th Ave.
New York 11, N.Y.

B. Herder Book Co.
15-17 S. Broadway
St. Louis 2, Mo.

Herder & Herder, Inc.
232 Madison Ave.
New York 16, N.Y.

Hillary House, Inc.
303 Park Ave. S.
New York 10, N.Y.

Hodder & Stoughton, Ltd.
St. Paul's House
20 Warwick Sq.
London, E. C. 4, England

Holt, Rinehart, & Winston, Inc.
383 Madison Ave.
New York 17, N.Y.

Johns Hopkins Press
Homewood
Baltimore 18, Md.

Humanities Press, Inc.
303 4th Ave.
New York 10, N.Y.

Jewish Publication Society of America
222 N. 15th St.
Philadelphia 2, Pa.

The Judson Press
Valley Forge, Pa.

P. J. Kenedy & Son
12 Barclay St.
New York 8, N.Y.

John Knox Press
8 N. 6th St.
Richmond 9, Va.

J. B. Lippincott Co.
E. Washington Sq.
Philadelphia 5, Pa.

The Liturgical Press
St. John's Abbey
Collegeville, Minn.

London House
   [*See* British Book Centre]

Longmans Green & Co., Ltd.
48 Grosvenor St.
London, W. 1, England

Gregory Lounz Books
11 East 45th St.
New York 17, N.Y.

Loyola Univ. Press
3441 N. Ashland Av.
Chicago 13, Ill.

Lutterworth Press
4 Bouverie St.
London, E. C. 4, England

David McCay Co.
119 W. 40th St.
New York 18, N.Y.

McClelland & Stewart, Ltd.
25 Holinger Rd.
Toronto 16, Ont., Canada

McGraw-Hill Book Co.
330 W. 42nd St.
New York 36, N.Y.

The Macmillan Co.
60 5th Ave.
New York 11, N.Y.

M.I.T. Press
Publications Office
77 Massachusetts Ave.
Cambridge 39, Mass.

Meridian Books, Inc.
C.O. World Publishing Co.
119 W. 57th St.
New York 19, N.Y.

Methuen & Co., Ltd.
36 Essex St. Strand
London, W. C. 2, England

Morehouse-Barlow Co., Inc.
14 E. 41st St.
New York 17, N.Y.

Muhlenberg Press
2900 Queen Lane
Philadelphia 29, Pa.

Thomas Nelson & Sons
18 E. 41st St.
New York 17, N.Y.

The Newman Press
69 W. Main St.
Westminster, Md.

The Noonday Press
19 Union Sq. W.
New York 3, N.Y.

W. W. Norton & Co.
55 5th Ave.
New York 3, N.Y.

Oliver & Boyd, Ltd.
39 Webeck St.
London, W. 1, England

Oxford Univ. Press
417 5th Ave.
New York 16, N.Y.

Pantheon Books, Inc.
22 E. 51st St.
New York 22, N.Y.

Paulist Press
Harristown Rd.
Glen Rock, N.J.

Penguin Books, Inc.
3300 Clipper Rd.
Baltimore 11, Md.

Philosophical Library Inc.
15 E. 40th St.
New York 16, N.Y.

Phoenix Books
  [*See* Univ. of Chicago Press]

Pontificio Instituto Biblico
Amministrazione Publicazioni
Piazza Pilotta, 35
Rome, 204, Italy

Frederick A. Praeger, Inc.
64 University Pl.
New York 3, N.Y.

Prentice-Hall, Inc.
Route 9W
Englewood Cliffs, N.J.

Princeton Univ. Press
Princeton, N.J.

The Priory Press
Asbury Rd.
Dubuque, Iowa

Quadrangle Books, Inc.
119 W. Lake St.
Chicago 1, Ill.

Rand McNally & Co.
Box 7600
Chicago 80, Ill.

Random House, Inc.
33 W. 60th St.
New York 23, N.Y.

H. Regnery Co.
E. Jackson Blvd.
Chicago 4, Ill.

Fleming H. Revell Co.
316 3rd Ave.
Westwood, N.J.

Rutgers Univ. Press
30 College Ave.
New Brunswick, N.J.

Ryerson Press
299 Queen St. W.
Toronto 2B, Ont., Canada

William H. Sadlier, Inc.
64 E. Lake St.
Chicago, Ill.

St. Anthony Guild Press
508 Marshall St.
Paterson 3, N.J.

St. Martin's Press
175 5th Ave.
New York 10, N.Y.

St. Paul Editions
50 St. Paul's Ave.
Jamaica Plain
Boston 30, Mass.

Scepter Press
30 N. LaSalle St.
Chicago 2, Ill.

Charles Scribner's Sons
597-599 5th Ave.
New York 17, N.Y.

The Seabury Press
1 Fawcett Pl.
Greenwich, Conn.

Sheed & Ward, Inc.
64 University Pl.
New York 3, N.Y.

Simon & Schuster, Inc.
630 5th Ave.
New York 20, N.Y.

Peter Smith
20 Railroad Ave.
Gloucester, Mass.

S.P.C.K. Press
Holy Trinity Church
Marylebone Rd.
London, N.W. 1, England

Stanford Univ. Press
Stanford, Calif.

Taplinger Publishing Co., Inc.
119 W. 57th St.
New York 19, N.Y.

Univ. of Chicago Press
5750 Ellis Ave.
Chicago, Ill.

University of Michigan Press
615 E. University Ave.
Ann Arbor, Mich.

Univ. of Notre Dame Press
Notre Dame, Ind.

The Viking Press, Inc.
625 Madison Ave.
New York 22, N.Y.

Joseph F. Wagner, Inc.
53 Park Pl.
New York 7, N.Y.

Westminster Press
Room 908 Witherspoon Bldg.
Walnut & Juniper Sts.
Philadelphia 7, Pa.

World Council of Churches
Geneva, Switzerland

The World Publishing Co.
2231 W. 110th St.
Cleveland 2, Ohio

Yale Univ. Press
149 York St.
New Haven 11, Conn.

Zondervan Publishing House
1415 Lake Drive S. E.
Grand Rapids 6, Mich.